LIVERPOOL FC
THE HISTORIC TREBLE

This is a Carlton Book

Published in association with Granada Media
Commercial Ventures

First published in 2001 by Carlton Books

10 9 8 7 6 5 4 3 2 1

First edition 2001

A CIP catalogue record for this book is available from the
British Library

ISBN 1 84222 455 7

Text, design and picture research by The Official Liverpool
Matchday Magazine

Photographic credits:
Allsport, Action Images, Empics, PA Photos, Steve Orino,
Mark Leech, Anton Want
Statistics supplied by Opta @ PLANETFOOTBALL.com

Printed and bound in Great Britain by Butler & Tanner,
Frome and London

Carlton Books Limited
20 Mortimer Street
London W1T 3JW

LIVERPOOL FC
THE HISTORIC TREBLE

OFFICIAL CELEBRATION

CARLTON
BOOKS

CONTENTS

GERARD HOULLIER

There is a big difference between dwelling on one's achievements and being proud of them. That is why, despite the success we all enjoyed at Liverpool in the 2000/2001 season, the only way to look is forward. However, this does not mean that the three cups we won, plus the Champions League place we managed to secure, should ever be forgotten. How could anyone forget that?

Those exploits may be history now. But, more importantly, they have gone down in history. Liverpool became the first club to win three finals in one season, and it may be some time before anyone does so again.

We do not intend to live on that season. We intend to build on it. But it is only fitting that what we achieved be immortalised in this wonderful book, which will be a constant reminder of what can be done through hard work and dedication.

Winning three cups was fantastic. We played 25 cup ties and lost only two. Usually when you have cup runs you lose points in the League. But we improved our consistency in the League because we finished very strongly.

Credit must be given to the players and to the backroom staff. They all pulled together to generate an excellent spirit. These players won three cups in 81 days. They played 63 games and scored 127 goals to become the third highest scorers in the club's history. That is magnificent.

For me, the key moment of the season was the game in Rome. Everyone was comparing us to the past and reminding us that Liverpool's last European trophy actually came in Rome against Roma. This, they said, was the acid test. But we went there and won. I thought then that if we got into the next round it would be a catalyst for the rest of the season because we would have laid a ghost. This result happened just before the Worthington Cup final, and on the back of it we won that first trophy.

As a Frenchman, winning the Uefa Cup probably gave me the greatest pleasure. If I were to ask my players, particularly the English, they would say the FA Cup meant most to them because every young Englishman dreams of playing in an FA Cup final.

Equally, I would have to say that the 'final' we played at Charlton Athletic

"THE KEY MOMENT OF THE SEASON FOR ME WAS THE VICTORY IN ROME"

on the last day of the season also gave me immense pleasure. Everyone knows that since the start of the campaign I had repeated that we wanted to improve on our previous year's Premiership position, which meant getting into the Champions League.

In the previous season we had finished fourth with 67 points. This time we finished third with 69 points, and we achieved the main objective we set at the start of the season. That's another sign of progress.

Finally, I want to say a big thank you to you, the supporters, who gave us fantastic support from the first game to the last, home and away. We could not have done what we did without your backing. You played as big a part as anyone in our success.

Long may it continue.

Ready to rumble: all lined up for the first Uefa Cup tie at Anfield

SATURDAY 19/8/00 TO THURSDAY 9/11/00

IN THE BEGINNING

picture mark leech

Three cups in one season. This is where it began. Bolstered by new signings Gary McAllister, Markus Babbel, Nick Barmby, Bernard Diomede and Pegguy Arphexad but missing the injured Robbie Fowler, the Reds kick off with five Premiership games in 22 days followed by their first steps back in Europe and the Worthington Cup. Solid League form and progress in the cups is imperative.

SATURDAY 19/8/00
BRADFORD CITY (H) PREMIERSHIP

MONDAY 21/8/00
ARSENAL (A) PREMIERSHIP

SATURDAY 26/8/00
SOUTHAMPTON (A) PREMIERSHIP

WEDNESDAY 6/9/00
ASTON VILLA (H) PREMIERSHIP

SATURDAY 9/9/00
MANCHESTER CITY (H) PREMIERSHIP

THURSDAY 14/9/00
RAPID BUCHAREST (A) UEFA CUP 1R 1L

SUNDAY 17/9/00
WEST HAM UNITED (A) PREMIERSHIP

SATURDAY 23/9/00
SUNDERLAND (H) PREMIERSHIP

THURSDAY 28/9/00
RAPID BUCHAREST (H) UEFA CUP 1R 2L

SUNDAY 1/10/00
CHELSEA (A) PREMIERSHIP

SUNDAY 15/10/00
DERBY COUNTY (A) PREMIERSHIP

SATURDAY 21/10/00
LEICESTER CITY (H) PREMIERSHIP

THURSDAY 26/10/00
SLOVAN LIBEREC (H) UEFA CUP 2R 1L

SUNDAY 29/10/00
EVERTON (H) PREMIERSHIP

WEDNESDAY 1/11/00
CHELSEA (H) WORTHINGTON CUP 3R

SATURDAY 4/11/00
LEEDS UNITED (A) PREMIERSHIP

THURSDAY 9/11/00
SLOVAN LIBEREC (A) UEFA CUP 2R 2L

RAPID BUCHAREST 0
LIVERPOOL 1 *Barmby 29*

LINE UP

1 LUCESCU
21 MUTICA
2 STANCIU
23 IENCSI
4 FRASINEANU
10 IFTODI
25 ISAILA
17 MALDARASANU
7 BUTA
16 CONSTANTIN
19 PANCU

SUBSTITUTES
18 BUNDEA
5 CHIRITA
13 BUGA
  Iftodi 73
6 CONSTANTINOVICI
20 SCHUMACHER
  Buta 46
12 RADULESCU
11 RADU
  Constantin 60

BOOKED
LUCESCU
SCHUMACHER

1 WESTERVELD
4 SONG
6 BABBEL
2 HENCHOZ
3 ZIEGE
20 BARMBY
16 HAMANN
23 CARRAGHER
24 DIOMEDE
10 OWEN
8 HESKEY

SUBSTITUTES
19 ARPHEXAD
14 HEGGEM
30 TRAORE
  Ziege 84
31 KIPPE
13 MURPHY
  Heskey 34
9 FOWLER
  Owen 80
18 MEIJER

BOOKED
HENCHOZ

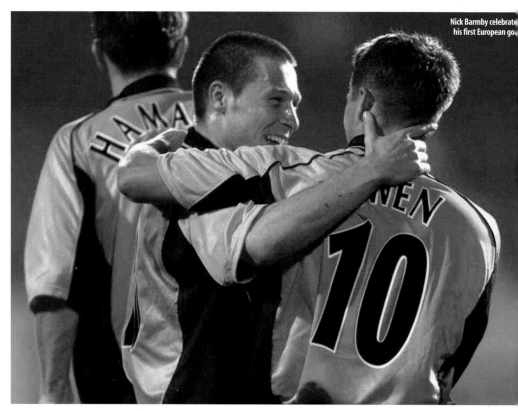

Nick Barmby celebrates his first European goal

Gérard Houllier's men returned to European competition after a season absent from the continent, aiming to re-establish the club's reputation outside domestic football.

Before the match, all the talk was of the European debut of Nick Barmby, who had crossed Stanley Park to sign for Liverpool in the summer. Despite playing regularly for his country, the England midfielder had missed out on European club action with his previous clubs Tottenham Hotspur, Middlesbrough and Everton.

"This is going to be an exciting new experience for me," said Barmby before the trip to Romania. "It's one of the main reasons I signed for Liverpool."

The attention paid to Barmby in the run-up to the tie turned out to be fully justified as he was the star on the night for Liverpool, kicking off a fantastic run of goalscoring in Europe to give the Reds a deserved first-leg lead.

Liverpool were almost punished early on when Christian Ziege was beaten by Maldarasanu, but the striker was unable to finish. Barmby struck the woodwork in the 29th minute, before Liverpool's pressure finally paid off with a goal. A superb piece of skill, speed and vision from Michael Owen set up the strike. Owen laid waste to virtually the entire Rapid Bucharest defence, thundering down the left wing before cutting inside. Shaping to shoot, he instead rolled the ball to the advancing Barmby who fired home his first goal for Liverpool with a sweet rising shot.

Houllier's men dominated from then on, with Dietmar Hamann and Bernard Diomede running the midfield, but failed to extend their lead. The Reds defence was never really examined in the second half and by the end it was frustrating that the margin of victory was just one goal.

"It was not easy, but this was still a most satisfying night's work," claimed Houllier. "We produced a highly professional performance when we needed one. I played an offensive side and it worked out."

34
The passes made by Nick Barmby to another Liverpool player

- **Nick Barmby strikes on European debut**
- **Hamann and Diomede boss the midfield**
- **Houllier hails a satisfying performance**

Michael OWEN
Emile HESKEY

Bernard DIOMEDE
Dietmar HAMANN
Jamie CARRAGHER
Nick BARMBY

Christian ZIEGE
Stephane HENCHOZ
Markus BABBEL
Rigobert SONG

Sander WESTERVELD

LIVERPOOL OFFICIAL MATCHDAY MAGAZINE
MAN OF THE MATCH MARKUS BABBEL

THOMMO'S VERDICT

"The emphasis in this match was on the defence after conceding two goals at home to Manchester City the previous Saturday, and we worked hard in training on tightening that up. We stressed that the players should be confident and were rewarded with a great European performance. It was a superb goal, Michael Owen's turn and run were incredible and Nick Barmby finished the move well.

"I think we should maybe have killed Rapid Bucharest off after that but you don't always get your own way in Europe and it was a magnificent away-leg performance. They were a good enough side, but I think in the end our determination and focus were too much for them. The defence performed excellently after all the work we had put in on the training ground, coming away with a satisfying clean sheet, and the result set us up well for the second leg at Anfield."

Babbel excelled at the heart of the defence

LIVERPOOL 0
RAPID BUCHAREST 0

LINE UP

1 WESTERVELD
14 HEGGEM
12 HYYPIA
6 BABBEL
30 TRAORE
17 GERRARD
16 HAMANN
15 BERGER
24 DIOMEDE
9 FOWLER
10 OWEN

SUBSTITUTES
19 ARPHEXAD
23 CARRAGHER
2 HENCHOZ
3 ZIEGE
   Traore 50
20 BARMBY
   Diomede 60
13 MURPHY
18 MEIJER

BOOKED
HAMANN

1 LUCESCU
2 STANCIU
4 FRASINEANU
5 CHIRITA
6 CONSTANTINOVICI
10 IFTODI
17 MALDARASANU
20 SCHUMACHER
23 IENCSI
25 ISAILA
19 PANCU

SUBSTITUTES
7 BUTA
18 BUNDEA
   Iftodi 55
14 BALAN
21 MUTICA
11 RADU
   Schumacher 65
16 CONSTANTIN
   Pancu 75
12 RADULESCU

BOOKED
CHIRITA, IENSCI

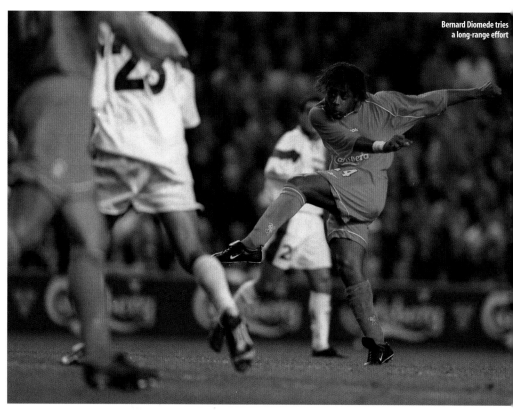

Bernard Diomede tries a long-range effort

Liverpool brought a slender one-goal lead back from Romania and, to the surprise of most fans, the anticipated stroll at Anfield turned into a nervy evening for the home side.

Manager Anghel Iordanescu had tightened up a Bucharest team that had posed little threat to Liverpool a fortnight earlier. The Romanians succeeded in stifling Liverpool's creativity in midfield and creating chances of their own.

Sander Westerveld was forced to produce an excellent save from Daniel Pancu in the first half. At the other end, a Dietmar Hamann free-kick hit the side netting and a Michael Owen chip, punched away by keeper Razvan Lucescu, were the best

chances of a frustrating 45 minutes for Liverpool. It was a much-changed starting line-up from the team that had drawn against Sunderland the previous Saturday and Robbie Fowler and Michael Owen, playing in tandem upfront for the first time in a year, were forced to feed on scraps for much of the game.

Nick Barmby and Christian Ziege were brought on to liven things up in the second half, but Liverpool were still unable to create many chances. Steven Gerrard, operating on the right-hand side of midfield, twice forced saves from the Romanian keeper from long range, and Fowler just failed to convert an enticing

Ziege cross. Even a flash of Michael Owen inspiration was denied when his run and shot on the break was cleared off the line by defender Constantinovici.

The Kop was relieved and dissatisfied as the whistle blew, but on a night that ended with Liverpool as the only English team left in the Uefa Cup, it was the result that mattered most.

"We struggled a bit and we were too predictable in the first half," admitted Gérard Houllier afterwards. "Rapid Bucharest made it very difficult for us, they had numbers in the midfield. To our credit we showed composure in keeping the result and we have achieved our aim, to go through."

69
The number of passes made by Sami Hyypia to his team-mates

Nervous Reds keep English flag flying
Owen and Fowler back together again
Mission accomplished says relieved boss

Robbie **FOWLER** Michael **OWEN**

Bernard **DIOMEDE** Patrik **BERGER** Dietmar **HAMANN** Steven **GERRARD**

Djimi **TRAORE** Sami **HYYPIA** Markus **BABBEL** Vegard **HEGGEM**

Sander **WESTERVELD**

LIVERPOOL OFFICIAL MATCHDAY MAGAZINE
MAN OF THE MATCH STEVEN GERRARD

THOMMO'S VERDICT

"We struggled a bit in this game but we managed to keep a clean sheet and with Nick Barmby's away goal under our belts from the first leg, that was always the main objective.

"Rapid Bucharest made things very difficult for us on the night. They are a neat side and they packed the midfield, but we always kept our composure. They came with a plan to frustrate us, they stuck to it well and we found it very difficult to create many chances.

"Michael Owen came very close to breaking the deadlock in the second half, as did Steven Gerrard, who was excellent in midfield for us. But we will fight another day and I think our football has a lot of room for improvement. We are through to the second round, we know we can get better and do very well in this competition. We don't fear anyone as we have the players to compete in Europe."

Steven Gerrard proved influential in midfield

LIVERPOOL 1 *Heskey 88*
SLOVAN LIBEREC 0

LINE UP

1 WESTERVELD
23 CARRAGHER
6 BABBEL
2 HENCHOZ
3 ZIEGE
7 SMICER
16 HAMANN
13 MURPHY
15 BERGER
8 HESKEY
9 FOWLER

SUBSTITUTES
19 ARPHEXAD
4 SONG
12 HYYPIA
30 TRAORE
21 McALLISTER
Murphy 69
20 BARMBY
Smicer 69
22 CAMARA

BOOKED
MURPHY, BABBEL

18 HAUZR
4 LEXA
22 PILNY
14 JOHANA
2 CAPEK
19 NEUMANN
17 JANU
3 MICHALIK
7 KOZUCH
8 STAJNER
9 LIUNI

SUBSTITUTES
5 BREDA
26 BENO
6 BAKES
Kozuch 83
10 JUN
Stajner 71
20 SILNY
23 BARTA
15 NEZMAR
Liuni 79

BOOKED
JOHANA

Stand back and admire Emile's volley...

Emile Heskey rescued a lacklustre Liverpool in the dying minutes with his fifth goal in three games as the Reds struggled to break down a resilient Czech side. But it was a night of frustration for Robbie Fowler as he continued his comeback after a 10-month injury lay-off.

In the first minute, his neat header from a Patrik Berger corner was saved by Slovan keeper Zbynek Hauzr, and it seemed the striker was feeling no affects from having spent the previous night at the birth of his second daughter. But a header over the bar from six yards following a pinpoint Smicer cross, a drive sent wide and a missed penalty indicated it wasn't to be Fowler's match.

The Czechs, well-marshalled in defence by Bohuslav Pilny and enterprising up front, put in a hard-working display, frequently stretching the Reds whose moves foundered on the edge of the Slovan penalty box too often, leading to a rash of reckless long-range shots missing the target.

A breakthrough looked to be on the cards when an innocuous challenge by Jirir Stajner on Dietmar Hamann in the 53rd minute was awarded with a penalty. But Fowler's kick sailed over the bar. Slovan almost took a shock lead 12 minutes later, when their Argentinian striker Lazzaro Liuni closed in on goal, but he was foiled by the excellent Markus Babbel.

It was the introduction of Gary McAllister and Nick Barmby to the midfield that finally made the difference to Liverpool and both were instrumental in the winner, two minutes from time. McAllister's floated corner was only half-cleared by Hauzr to Barmby's and his ball across the face of goal found Heskey who finished emphatically from six yards out.

"Robbie could have had two or three but we must indulge him and be patient," Gérard Houllier said. "The goals will come, there was plenty of movement from Robbie and he was getting in the right positions."

13

The total blocks, clearances and tackles made by Stephane Henchoz

- Emile gets winner two minutes from time
- Hardworking Czechs stifle Reds midfield
- Robbie misses penalty in front of the Kop

Robbie FOWLER · **Emile HESKEY**

Patrik BERGER · **Dietmar HAMANN** · **Danny MURPHY** · **Vladimir SMICER**

Christian ZIEGE · **Stephane HENCHOZ** · **Markus BABBEL** · **Jamie CARRAGHER**

Sander WESTERVELD

LIVERPOOL OFFICIAL MATCHDAY MAGAZINE
MAN OF THE MATCH **EMILE HESKEY**

THOMMO'S VERDICT

"This was an extremely difficult game for us as we knew it would be. They packed the midfield and marked us man for man.

"For our part, our football was not fluid enough. We had three or four really good chances but we didn't manage to convert any of them and so we left it very late. Of course, if Robbie had scored the penalty it would have been a different story but these things happen.

"The most vital aspect of the home fixture in Europe is to keep a clean sheet and we did that, and did it well, and we must remember that we do go over there with a goal lead.

"Emile Heskey worked tirelessly upfront and he was extremely sharp. When the ball was played through to him from Nicky Barmby I thought it might have been a chance gone begging but luckily he was lively and rifled it into the back of the net."

...and salute the vital breakthrough

LIVERPOOL 2 *Murphy 11 Fowler 104 after extra time*
CHELSEA 1 *Zola 29*

LINE UP

19 ARPHEXAD
23 CARRAGHER
12 HYYPIA
2 HENCHOZ
30 TRAORE
20 BARMBY
16 HAMANN
13 MURPHY
15 BERGER
7 SMICER
8 FOWLER

SUBSTITUTES
1 WESTERVELD
4 SONG
3 ZIEGE
Traore 85
21 McALLISTER
Barmby 93
8 HESKEY
Smicer 83

BOOKED
TRAORE
MURPHY
HESKEY

SENT OFF
HESKEY

1 DE GOEY
3 BABAYARO
6 DESAILLY
7 BOGARDE
9 HASSELBAINK
10 JOKANOVIC
11 WISE
15 MELCHIOT
19 FLO
25 ZOLA
26 TERRY

SUBSTITUTES
23 CUDICINI
24 DALLA BONA
22 GUDJOHNSEN
Babayaro 65
20 MORRIS
Terry 88
8 POYET
Flo 82

BOOKED
JOKANOVIC

Rejoice! For God hath scored upon his return

- **Robbie's first goal in 11 months seals it**
- **Heskey off in bad-tempered encounter**
- **Murphy on target as Reds gain revenge**

LIVERPOOL 2 *Murphy 11 Fowler 104 after extra time*
CHELSEA 1 *Zola 29*

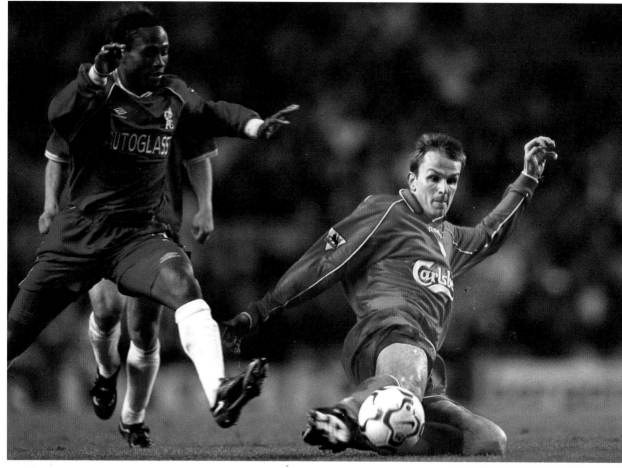

Robbie Fowler netted his first goal in 11 months on a stormy night to settle this third-round Worthington Cup tie at Anfield.

But Fowler's achievement was overshadowed by a controversial red card for Emile Heskey in the final minute of extra time after an innocuous clash with Dutch midfielder Winston Bogarde.

"I thought Emile was unlucky," said Gérard Houllier afterwards, "because he was being elbowed by Bogarde and raised an arm to protect himself."

Liverpool were seeking revenge over Claudio Ranieri's men, after their 3-0 defeat in the Premiership at Stamford Bridge a month earlier. And they made a perfect start, taking the lead in the 11th minute. Didi Hamann picked out Danny Murphy with an accurate right-foot flick on the edge of the box. Murphy had time and space to steady himself before rifling a precise shot past Ed De Goey and into the bottom corner.

But Chelsea conjured an equaliser from nowhere in the 29th minute. A neat reverse ball into the area from Tore Andre Flo enabled Celestine Babayaro to cross from the left to Gianfranco Zola, who was allowed to rise unchallenged between Sami Hyypia and Djimi Traore to head home.

Fowler came close to restoring Liverpool's advantage in the 77th minute, latching on to a Murphy pass, only to see his driven shot hit the post. Patrik Berger and Heskey also went close.

Finally, 14 minutes into extra time, Fowler took a pass from Berger in his stride, cutting in from the right before slotting a left-foot shot into the bottom corner from 15 yards to earn the Reds a trip to Stoke.

Dietmar Hamann beats Celestine Babayaro to the ball in a fiery cup tie

9

The number of shots fired by Robbie Fowler during the match

"Say what you like about Robbie Fowler, he never, ever hides and even though his form may have deserted him, his class never will"

David Maddock *The Mirror*

Danny Murphy is congratulated by Hamann on his neat finish

DO THEY MEAN US?

ROBBIE'S ROCKET RETURN
Fowler ends drought

"Say what you like about Fowler, he never, ever hides, never ever takes the easy option, even when his finishing goes wonky. It is a question of class and, even though his form may have deserted him, that never will"
David Maddock
The Mirror

"I liked the spirit of this game because both teams went out to win and unfortunately we didn't. All the compliments go to Liverpool"
Claudio Ranieri

"Somewhere amid the madness of this tie, Robbie Fowler reminded his detractors that, like riding a bike, scoring a goal is an art that, once learned, is never forgotten"
Ian Ross *The Guardian*

Fowler scores!
Robbie ends his drought then Heskey sees red as tempers boil

"The winning habit that Liverpool have acquired recently has engendered a surge of confidence. They threatened to run riot briefly and Fowler's goal was greeted by frenzied celebrations"
Oliver Kay *The Times*

LIVERPOOL OFFICIAL MATCHDAY MAGAZINE
MAN OF THE MATCH DANNY MURPHY

Robbie FOWLER
Vladimir SMICER

Patrik BERGER
Danny MURPHY
Dietmar HAMANN
Nick BARMBY

Djimi TRAORE
Sami HYYPIA
Stephane HENCHOZ
Jamie CARRAGHER

Pegguy ARPHEXAD

THOMMO'S VERDICT

"They'd hurt our pride with the 3-0 defeat at Stamford Bridge a month earlier and we had something to prove. We made a great start, taking the lead with a fine strike from Danny Murphy who had an outstanding game. We then let Chelsea back into it and Zola's goal was a little disappointing from a defensive point of view.

"Beforehand some people had been underestimating this competition but you could see the commitment from both sides. It was a typical cup tie – fast, full of commitment and both sides played well.

"As the game wore on it became very frustrating for Robbie Fowler who didn't seem to be getting his just rewards for all his hard work over the last few games. But his reaction after scoring the winner for us said it all really. His fitness was excellent, and he was still running away well into extra time. It marked Robbie's return."

SLOVAN LIBEREC 2 *Stajner 9 Breda 85*
LIVERPOOL 3 *Barmby 31 Heskey 75 Owen 82*

LINE UP

18 HAUZR
2 CAPEK
3 MICHALIK
4 LEXA
8 STAJNER
9 LIUNI
10 JUN
14 JOHANA
17 JANU
19 NEUMANN
22 PILNY

SUBSTITUTES
6 BAKES
11 ZABOJNIK
5 BREDA
Michalik 83
7 KOZUCH
Liuni 73
13 VIDLICKA
15 NEZMAR
23 BARTA

BOOKED
JOHANA

1 WESTERVELD
23 CARRAGHER
6 BABBEL
12 HYYPIA
3 ZIEGE
7 SMICER
17 GERRARD
16 HAMANN
20 BARMBY
8 HESKEY
9 FOWLER

SUBSTITUTES
1 ARPHEXAD
30 TRAORE
4 SONG
2 HENCHOZ
21 McALLISTER
Fowler 63
13 MURPHY
Carragher 55
10 OWEN
Hamann 82

BOOKED
ZIEGE
SMICER

Two rounds, two goals for Barmby in Europe

Michael Owen made a stunning impact on this second-leg tie, scoring a sublime goal just 20 seconds after coming on as a second-half substitute to add to strikes by Nick Barmby and Emile Heskey that saw Liverpool march into the third round of the Uefa Cup.

There were a few scares along the way though, and Ladislav Skorpil's well-drilled Slovan threatened as early as the sixth minute. Jari Stajner was given too much room on the left and his intelligent pass gave Lazzaro Luini, holding off Markus Babbel, a chance that he dragged across the goal. Three minutes later, they were level on aggregate. Roman Jun skipped past Jamie Carragher on the left, before centring for Stajner, who outjumped Christian Ziege to head beyond Sander Westerveld.

It was the jolt Liverpool needed. Gerrard and Heskey both unleashed long-range efforts, before Ziege's pinpoint free-kick was met by Barmby, who glanced the ball through a sea of players and in off the post on the half hour.

Slovan weren't finished, however, and Stajner again wriggled through the Reds defence only to see his low cross evade Luini's desperate lunge.

Emile Heskey came close to scoring a couple of times before finally getting on the scoresheet in the 76th minute when he met a Vladimir Smicer centre and acrobatically fired a close-range shot which was just too hot for Hauzr to hold.

Owen's introduction as an 82nd-minute substitute for Dietmar Hamann was still being announced when he swivelled on to a half chance 25 yards out and curled his shot unerringly into the top corner.

Slovan pulled one back three minutes later to test the travelling contingent's nerves, when the substitute David Breda followed Owen in scoring with his first touch.

"It was a difficult game," said Gérard Houllier. "We created most of the scares for ourselves, but Liberec also made it hard."

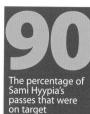

90
The percentage of Sami Hyypia's passes that were on target

- Barmby hits the net again in Europe
- Sub Owen strikes in just 20 seconds
- Heskey too hot for Slovan to handle

Robbie FOWLER   Emile HESKEY

Vladimir SMICER   Dietmar HAMANN   Steven GERRARD   Nick BARMBY

Christian ZIEGE   Sami HYYPIA   Markus BABBEL   Jamie CARRAGHER

Sander WESTERVELD

LIVERPOOL OFFICIAL MATCHDAY MAGAZINE MAN OF THE MATCH: STEVEN GERRARD

THOMMO'S VERDICT

"We'd been hearing whispers from the Czech Republic that Slovan Liberec were fancying their chances at home, and we gave them the respect they deserved. People in Britain hadn't heard of them before, so presumed they weren't very good, but they were a strong outfit. The lads showed plenty of composure after Slovan scored the opening goal. We didn't panic and kept our shape, and by the end of the night it was a very pleasing win.

"We don't need telling it was bad for us to concede goals, it was upsetting and we worked hard on the defence on the training ground. On a more positive note, Michael Owen's goal so soon after coming off the bench was quite incredible, and Emile Heskey was superb all evening. He put up with some atrocious fouling from the players and even worse abuse from the crowd but he kept his cool and took his goal well."

Steven Gerrard: influential in the Reds engine room

GOALS GALORE

Liverpool's previously watertight defence is uncharacteristically porous as they leak goals in all but three of their opening 12 league games. Anfield is still a fortress, with 16 points won out of 18, but on their travels the Reds concede 13 in six matches. By the start of November, Liverpool lie fourth.

FA CARLING PREMIERSHIP

SATURDAY 19/8/00
LIVERPOOL 1 Heskey 67
BRADFORD CITY 0

MONDAY 21/8/00
ARSENAL 2 Lauren 38, Henry 89
LIVERPOOL 0

SATURDAY 26/8/00
SOUTHAMPTON 3 Pahars 73 90, El-Khalej 84
LIVERPOOL 3 Owen 23 64, Hyypia 55

WEDNESDAY 6/9/00
LIVERPOOL 3 Owen 5 12 33
ASTON VILLA 1 Stone 83

SATURDAY 6/9/00
LIVERPOOL 3 Owen 1, Hamann 56 81
MANCHESTER CITY 2 Weah 67, Horlock 81pen

SUNDAY 17/9/00
WEST HAM UNITED 1 Di Canio 69pen
LIVERPOOL 1 Gerrard 12

SATURDAY 23/9/00
SUNDERLAND 1 Phillips 14
LIVERPOOL 1 Owen 34

SUNDAY 1/10/00
CHELSEA 3 Westerveld10og, Hasselbaink 11, Gudjohnsen 71
LIVERPOOL 0

SUNDAY 15/10/00
DERBY COUNTY 0
LIVERPOOL 4 Heskey 17 54 67, Berger 80

SATURDAY 21/10/00
LIVERPOOL 1 Heskey 69
LEICESTER CITY 0

SUNDAY 29/10/00
LIVERPOOL 3 Barmby 12, Heskey 56, Berger 78pen
EVERTON 1 Campbell 17

SATURDAY 4/11/00
LEEDS UNITED 4 Viduka 24,46,73,75
LIVERPOOL 3 Hyypia 2, Ziege 17, Smicer 61

Would the gods be on his
side at home and abroad?

HEAVEN SCENT

While Patrik Berger joins skipper Jamie Redknapp on the specialist's table, and Sven Goran Eriksson is appointed England coach, the Reds gear up for eight Premiership games before the turn of the year plus a further two Worthington Cup ties and a 3,304-mile round-trip to Athens. Three games in a week is becoming routine. Meanwhile, there's praise for the increasingly influential Steven Gerrard from an old favourite. "The kid can play virtually anywhere," says Alan Hansen. "He's been magnificent. It looks like he might not be able to play 50 games a season but if anybody is ever going to be the complete player, it's Gerrard."

SUNDAY 12/11/00
COVENTRY CITY (H) **PREMIERSHIP**

SUNDAY 19/11/00
TOTTENHAM HOTSPUR (A) **PREMIERSHIP**

THURSDAY 23/11/00
OLYMPIAKOS (A) **UEFA CUP 3R 1L**

SUNDAY 26/11/00
NEWCASTLE UNITED (A) **PREMIERSHIP**

WEDNESDAY 29/11/00
STOKE CITY (A) **WORTHINGTON CUP 4R**

SATURDAY 2/12/00
CHARLTON ATHLETIC (H) **PREMIERSHIP**

THURSDAY 7/12/00
OLYMPIAKOS (H) **UEFA CUP 3R 2L**

SUNDAY 10/12/00
IPSWICH TOWN (H) **PREMIERSHIP**

WEDNESDAY 13/12/00
FULHAM (H) **WORTHINGTON CUP 5R**

SUNDAY 17/12/00
MANCHESTER UNITED (A) **PREMIERSHIP**

SATURDAY 23/12/00
ARSENAL (H) **PREMIERSHIP**

TUESDAY 26/12/00
MIDDLESBROUGH (A) **PREMIERSHIP**

OLYMPIAKOS 2 *Alexandris 65 90*
LIVERPOOL 2 *Barmby 38 Gerrard 68*

LINE UP

31 ELEFTHEROPOULOS
32 ANATOLAKIS
23 KONTIS
5 AMANATIDIS
14 MAVROGENIDIS
2 PATSATZOGLOU
6 POURSANIDIS
11 DJORDJEVIC
20 ZETTERBERG
30 ALEXANDRIS
10 GIOVANNI

SUBSTITUTES
1 GEORGIOU
3 KARATAIDIS
19 KOSTOULAS
17 PASSALIS
21 GEORGATOS
Zetterberg 71
7 GIANNAKOPOULOS
Mavrogenidis 56
8 LUCIANO
Poursanidis 45

1 WESTERVELD
23 CARRAGHER
6 BABBEL
12 HYYPIA
30 TRAORE
20 BARMBY
17 GERRARD
16 HAMANN
13 MURPHY
8 HESKEY
10 OWEN

SUBSTITUTES
19 ARPHEXAD
2 HENCHOZ
5 STAUNTON
Traore 45
4 SONG
21 McALLISTER
Murphy 90
28 PARTRIDGE
7 SMICER
Owen 65

BOOKED
TRAORE
BABBEL
MURPHY

Nick Barmby stuns the crowd with his strike

The Reds were just seconds away from an impressive victory against the Greek champions in a passionate Olympic Stadium. It was still an impressive first-leg result to take back to Anfield, but the tie could and should have been wrapped up on the night as the Reds proved superior in every department to a side who had gone 15 Champions League home matches without defeat.

Unnerved by the smoke bombs that met their arrival in the arena, Liverpool looked solid at the back and played some intelligent football. In the 38th minute they stunned the Greeks with a brilliant opportunist goal. Jamie Carragher's throw was flicked on by Emile Heskey and Nick Barmby swept the ball beyond Eleftheropoulos into the net to silence the crowd. They almost grabbed a second six minutes after the break when Heskey raced on to a long ball on the right and sent in a low cross for Michael Owen. He missed it but Barmby sprinted in from the left only to hook his shot against the woodwork.

Olympiakos levelled on 65 minutes. Giovanni's cross was met by Alexios Alexandris, whose spectacular scissors kick from 12 yards eluded the grasp of Sander Westerveld.

But Liverpool hit back just three minutes later, when Barmby swung in a cross from the left and Steven Gerrard rose above the Greek defence to head powerfully into the net. Steve Staunton, on as a substitute for Djimi Traore, then rattled the bar with a curling free-kick. On 83 minutes, Vladimir Smicer was allowed to run from the halfway line but with only the keeper to beat, his weak shot hit the post.

The match was in stoppage time when Alexandris hit his second, volleying home Giovanni's flicked header after a rare defensive lapse by Markus Babbel.

"The amount of chances we created shows how far we are progressing as a team," said Barmby. "The tie is not dead yet, we will have to keep our heads down and our mouths shut, but we are confident after tonight."

34 The number of passes made by Nick Barmby to his team-mates

- ■ **Barmby fires opener to silence crowd**
- ■ **Gerrard's powerful header makes it two**
- ■ **Staunton rattles the Greek woodwork**

Emile HESKEY · Michael OWEN
Danny MURPHY · Dietmar HAMANN · Steven GERRARD · Nick BARMBY
Djimi TRAORE · Sami HYYPIA · Markus BABBEL · Jamie CARRAGHER
Sander WESTERVELD

LIVERPOOL OFFICIAL MATCHDAY MAGAZINE
MAN OF THE MATCH EMILE HESKEY

THOMMO'S VERDICT

"It was one of the best 90 minutes of football any Liverpool team has played away from home in Europe. It was a fantastic game in a hostile atmosphere against a team unbeaten at home and a side that had one of the best home records in Europe.

"We dug in all evening and the players were so focused. Steven Gerrard and Nick Barmby both took their goals extremely well and we controlled the game, limiting their chances.

"We would have taken 2-2 before the game but the atmosphere in the dressing room after the match was very quiet because of the last-minute equaliser. We knew we should have done much better and come away with the victory. We hit the woodwork, we had some other great chances and we should have wrapped it up on the night. Having said that, the result set us up for an exciting return leg at Anfield."

Emile Heskey rampages through the rearguard

STOKE CITY 0
LIVERPOOL 8
Ziege 6   Smicer 26   Babbel 28   Fowler 39 82 85 pen   Hyypia 59   Murphy 65

LINE UP

14 MUGGLETON
2 HANSSON
15 DORIGO
5 MOHAN
6 GUNNARSSON
7 GUDJONSSON
8 KAVANAGH
4 RISOM
3 CLARKE
9 THORNE
12 LIGHTBOURNE

SUBSTITUTES
28 NEAL
31 KRISTINSSON
18 PETTY
Hansson 22
19 THORDARSON
Lightbourne 76
29 GOODFELLOW
Thorne 76

19 ARPHEXAD
2 HENCHOZ
3 ZIEGE
6 BABBEL
12 HYYPIA
7 SMICER
13 MURPHY
21 McALLISTER
23 CARRAGHER
9 FOWLER
28 PARTRIDGE

SUBSTITUTES
1 WESTERVELD
29 WRIGHT
Babbel 45
16 HAMANN
Smicer 74
20 BARMBY
Patridge 67
8 HESKEY

BOOKED
ZIEGE
HENCHOZ

Vladimir Smicer's creative running was rewarded with a goal

- **Potters crushed by Reds' eight-goal avalanche**
- **Partridge and Wright make their senior debuts**
- **Babbel nets the first goal of his Anfield career**

STOKE CITY 0
LIVERPOOL 8 *Ziege 6   Smicer 26   Babbel 28   Fowler 39 82 85 pen   Hyypia 59   Murphy 65*

A solid backline jumps as one to keep out Stoke

A commanding Liverpool performance at the Britannia Stadium helped the Reds rack up their biggest away win in 104 years and make it into the last eight of the Worthington Cup.

Stoke striker Peter Thorne hit the post in the third minute following a mistake by Liverpool reserve keeper Pegguy Arphexad but three minutes later the Reds were off the mark when Robbie Fowler curled in a pinpoint cross for Christian Ziege to hit a half-volley past Carl Muggleton.

Liverpool, with Richie Partridge and Steven Wright making their senior debuts, went 2-0 up in the 25th minute, when Markus Babbel's long ball sent Vladimir Smicer clear and he guided a shot into the corner. Three minutes later, Babbel himself netted the first goal of his Anfield career to make it 3-0.

Liverpool's fourth came six minutes before the break, when Gary McAllister's corner was flicked on by Sami Hyypia and Fowler nodded home. Hyypia bagged the fifth 15 minutes after the restart when he prodded home a Danny Murphy cross.

Soon after, Christian Ziege's through ball left Stoke's defence in tatters and Fowler squared it to Murphy to make it six. In the 81st minute Fowler latched on to a Ziege pass before drilling a low shot unerringly past Muggleton from 20 yards. Minutes later, Nick Barmby was upended by the Stoke keeper and Fowler dispatched the penalty to secure his hat-trick and make it eight. But the electronic scoreboard, confused by the rout, flashed up 9-0. It was Robbie's 25th goal in 29 League Cup appearances.

"It was embarrassing," groaned Stoke captain Tony Dorigo. "We let ourselves down. But they were impressively ruthless."

10

The number of shots Liverpool had on target, including their eight goals

Fowler's running off the ball and selfless distribution helped to create goals. On this evidence, an England call-up is surely imminent"

avid McVay *The Times*

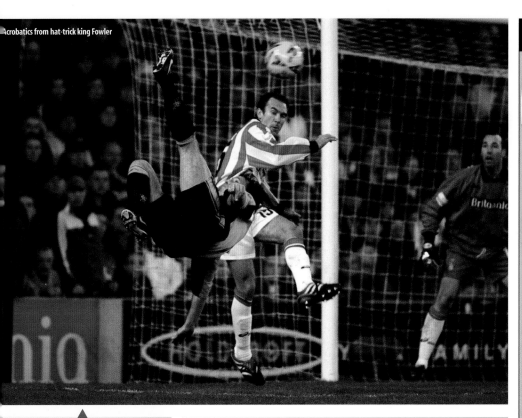

Acrobatics from hat-trick king Fowler

IVERPOOL OFFICIAL MATCHDAY MAGAZINE
AN OF THE MATCH **ROBBIE FOWLER**

Robbie **FOWLER** Richie **PARTRIDGE**

Jamie **CARRAGHER** Gary **McALLISTER** Danny **MURPHY** Vladimir **SMICER**

Christian **ZIEGE** Sami **HYYPIA** Stephane **HENCHOZ** Markus **BABBEL**

Pegguy **ARPHEXAD**

THOMMO'S VERDICT

"Stoke should have scored in the opening moments of this game when Pegguy Arphexad made an error but luckily for us it bounced back into his hands and we got away with it.

"From there on in we dominated the game in front of a fervent Stoke support and at this point in our season

it was inevitable someone was going to get a good hiding given the run of results we'd been having – it was unlucky for Stoke it was them. We had everything here: well-worked goals, progressive possession and a solid defence.

"It was very nice to have a game like this in the Cup but

we were aware at the same time that we needed to transfer this kind of solidity into our Premiership games.

"Robbie was obviously the highlight of the night, getting involved in six of the goals. Markus Babbel got on the scoresheet too. It was a tremendous display all round."

LIVERPOOL 2 *Heskey 27 Barmby 59*
OLYMPIAKOS 0

LINE UP

1 WESTERVELD
6 BABBEL
2 HENCHOZ
12 HYYPIA
23 CARRAGHER
20 BARMBY
17 GERRARD
16 HAMANN
13 MURPHY
7 SMICER
8 HESKEY

SUBSTITUTES
19 ARPHEXAD
29 WRIGHT
3 ZIEGE
 Murphy 77
21 McALLISTER
 Gerrard 90
28 PARTRIDGE
9 FOWLER
10 OWEN

BOOKED
ZIEGE

31 ELEFTHEROPOULOS
32 ANATOLAKIS
5 AMANATIDIS
6 POURSANIDIS
21 GEORGATOS
11 DJORDJEVIC
2 PATSATZOGLOU
20 ZETTERBERG
14 MAVROGENIDIS
10 GIOVANNI
30 ALEXANDRIS

SUBSTITUTES
1 GEORGIOU
3 KARATAIDIS
19 KOSTOULAS
23 KONTIS
4 NINIADIS
 Patsatzoglou 63
8 LUCIANO
 Mavrogenidis 53
24 OFORI QUAYE
 Zetterberg 63

BOOKED
ELEFTHEROPOULOS
NINIADIS

Sami Hyypia makes an acrobatic clearance

Nick Barmby and Emile Heskey maintained their impressive form in the Uefa Cup to dispatch the Greek champions and fire Liverpool into the last 16.

It was the Reds' most assured performance in Europe so far, with none of the sloppiness that had marred the earlier rounds, and there was only ever going to be one team that progressed.

Steven Gerrard came close to scoring a marvellous goal as early as the fifth minute, only for Dimitris Eleftheropoulos to make a gravity-defying leap to palm his 20-yard dipping volley over the bar.

Olympiakos rarely threatened although Sami Hyypia was forced to hack a cross from Predrag Djordevic away from Alexios Alexandris as Sander Westerveld hesitated.

Liverpool took the lead on 28 minutes. The tenacious Gerrard won the ball and fed Nick Barmby, who sprang the offside trap with a pass that released Emile Heskey. The £11million striker drew the keeper and steadied himself before finding the corner of the net to score his third goal in this season's competition.

Four minutes later, Barmby, chasing a through ball, darted through midfield, only to be scythed down by the Greek keeper who was lucky to receive only a yellow card.

Liverpool stepped up a gear after the interval, and Barmby seemed to have a hand in almost everything they did. His corner was picked out by Hyypia, whose header left Eleftheropoulos for dead, but it was cleared off the line by Grigorios Georgatos. The summer signing from Everton put the tie beyond doubt on the hour. Danny Murphy played a superb through ball to Barmby, who skipped round the onrushing Eleftheropoulos to fire home with composure from an acute angle with a shot that clipped the near post.

Westerveld was lucky to escape a caution when he pulled down Djordjevic, but there was no denying Liverpool deserved their 4-2 aggregate victory and a place in the fourth-round draw.

81 The percentage of perfect passes from Jamie Carragher out of defence

- **Champs League outcasts put to sword**
- **Heskey nets his third European goal**
- **Barmby seals passage into next round**

Emile HESKEY — Vladimir SMICER

Danny MURPHY — Dietmar HAMANN — Steven GERRARD — Nick BARMBY

Jamie CARRAGHER — Sami HYYPIA — Stephane HENCHOZ — Markus BABBEL

Sander WESTERVELD

LIVERPOOL OFFICIAL MATCHDAY MAGAZINE
MAN OF THE MATCH **EMILE HESKEY**

THOMMO'S VERDICT

"We knew this game was going to be very different to how the first leg had been over in Athens, as we were well aware that Olympiakos could play a lot better than they had done then.

"They came over to Anfield on the back of three wins and with a new bloke in charge, so they were confident they could put one over on us.

"On the night, every one of our lads was exceptional – in their attitude, their commitment and their effort. Our movement and passing were good and when Emile Heskey scored on the half hour it basically knocked the stuffing out of them.

"Saying that, though, they came out in the second half with a renewed urgency and played some good football but then Nicky Barmby's strike finished them off. A superb victory that meant we could go into the domestic Christmas season full of confidence."

Emile Heskey kept up his excellent form

LIVERPOOL 3 *Owen 105 Smicer 113 Barmby 120 after extra time*
FULHAM 0

LINE UP

LIVERPOOL
1 WESTERVELD
2 HENCHOZ
6 BABBEL
12 HYYPIA
23 CARRAGHER
7 SMICER
13 MURPHY
17 GERRARD
25 BISCAN
8 HESKEY
9 FOWLER

SUBSTITUTES
26 NIELSEN
27 VIGNAL
20 BARMBY
Heskey 96
21 McALLISTER
Gerrard 115
10 OWEN
Fowler 74

FULHAM
1 TAYLOR
2 FINNAN
3 BREVETT
4 MELVILLE
5 COLEMAN
8 CLARK
15 HAYLES
19 GOLDBAEK
20 SAHA
23 DAVIS
25 FERNANDES

SUBSTITUTES
6 SYMONS
7 TROLLOPE
22 BOA MORTE
Hayles 91
12 HAHNEMANN
40 STOLCERS
Fernandes 91

BOOKING
BOA MORTE

Vladimir Smicer goes close with this effort

It took extra time to separate them, but Gérard Houllier emerged victorious in the battle of the French managers at a rain-sodden Anfield.

Jean Tigana's Nationwide League leaders outplayed the Reds for long periods of this fifth-round tie and Liverpool had to rely on their superior determination and physical strength to reach the last four.

Robbie Fowler, hat-trick hero in the previous round, had a disappointing night save for one cheeky 20-yard chip, and was substituted for Michael Owen in the 76th minute. Debutant Igor Biscan came close to scoring after eight minutes, steering in a long shot that smashed against Sean Davis and went inches wide, while Emile Heskey wasted several opportunities in the first half.

Meanwhile Fulham almost took the lead on 14 minutes, when Sami Hyypia's backpass fell short, forcing Sander Westerveld to rush off the line. His clearance rebounded off Lee Clark, but fortunately he ballooned wide.

Tigana's side continued to pose a threat after the break, with Clark dominant in midfield, while Westerveld was forced to smother a stinging drive from Bjarne Goldbaek on the hour mark.

But Liverpool ended the 90 minutes the stronger, Danny Murphy striking a free-kick against the Fulham woodwork.

Fifteen minutes into extra-time the deadlock was broken when a deep cross from Vladimir Smicer was met by a header from Owen. Taylor saved with his feet but the rebound trickled back to Owen, who smashed home to celebrate his 21st birthday a day early.

Six minutes from the end, Nick Barmby fed Smicer, who drove home the second with his right, and Barmby himself finished off a wonderful 40-yard run, skipping past three challenges, by driving home the third under Taylor's body in the dying seconds.

80
The percentage of dribbles performed successfully by Vladimir Smicer

■ **Owen comes off bench to break deadlock**
■ **Brilliant Smicer drives home Reds' second**
■ **Barmby's 40-yard run rounds off victory**

Robbie FOWLER
Emile HESKEY

Igor BISCAN
Danny MURPHY
Steven GERRARD
Vladimir SMICER

Jamie CARRAGHER
Sami HYYPIA
Stephane HENCHOZ
Markus BABBEL

Sander WESTERVELD

LIVERPOOL OFFICIAL MATCHDAY MAGAZINE
MAN OF THE MATCH STEVEN GERRARD

THOMMO'S VERDICT

"We knew it would be a tricky game. In many ways, Fulham are a similar side to Ipswich Town, who we had lost to the previous Sunday. They pass the ball neatly and quickly in triangles, and it was obvious even then that they'd be promoted.

"We gave them plenty of respect but for all their possession, they failed to get in behind us and do any damage.

"We'd have liked to have got the job done in 90 minutes, especially with the Manchester United game coming up on the following Sunday, but once extra time came around we played really well and dominated. Nick Barmby and Michael Owen coming on gave us impetus and once the first goal went in their heads went down.

"It was nice for Vladimir Smicer to get his first goal at Anfield and Igor Biscan had an excellent full debut for us, playing really well in midfield for two hours of football."

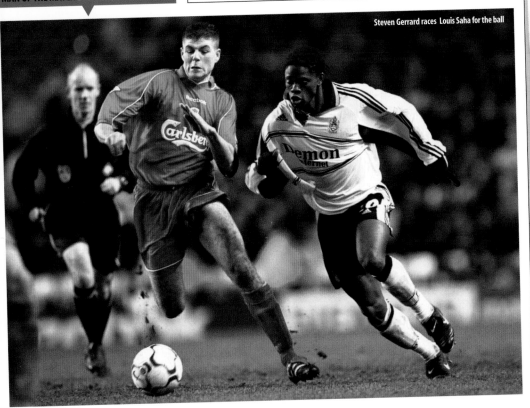

Steven Gerrard races Louis Saha for the ball

Instant legend status – just add wonder goal at Old Trafford

Igor Biscan arrives as the Reds face 13 games between mid-November and the end of the year. In between their Greek odyssey and Worthington Cup rout of Stoke, they stumble in consecutive away games in North London and Tyneside. But the boss refuses to change his tactics: "We win as a team and lose as a team. We'll continue to place the emphasis on attack." In-form Ipswich Town end a 10-game unbeaten home run, but Danny Murphy's fantastic free-kick at Old Trafford marks Gérard Houllier's 100th game in charge in style and Arsenal are blitzed at Anfield six days later.

FA CARLING PREMIERSHIP

SUNDAY 12/11/00
LIVERPOOL 4 McAllister 13, Gerrard 51, Heskey 82 87
COVENTRY CITY 1 Thompson 56

SUNDAY 19/11/00
TOTTENHAM HOTSPUR 2 Ferdinand 32, Sherwood 41
LIVERPOOL 1 Fowler 18

SUNDAY 26/11/00
NEWCASTLE UNITED 2 Solano 4, Dyer 70
LIVERPOOL 1 Heskey 78

SATURDAY 2/12/00
LIVERPOOL 3 Fish 5og, Heskey 78, Babbel 90
CHARLTON ATHLETIC 0 Fish 5og

SUNDAY 10/12/00
LIVERPOOL 0
IPSWICH TOWN 1 Stewart 45

SUNDAY 17/12/00
MANCHESTER UNITED 0
LIVERPOOL 1 Murphy 43

SATURDAY 23/12/00
LIVERPOOL 4 Gerrard 11, Owen 61, Barmby 70, Fowler 90
ARSENAL 0

TUESDAY 26/12/00
MIDDLESBROUGH 1 Karembeu 41
LIVERPOOL 0

TAKE THAT AND PARTY

CHAMPAGNE ON ICE

Tell me ma, me ma: the
Kop has Cardiff in its sights

New Year's Day finds the Reds fifth in the table, drawn at home to Rotherham United in the third round of the FA Cup and already in sight of Cardiff's Millennium Stadium – Crystal Palace stand between them and a place in the Worthington Cup final. The Uefa Cup doesn't resume until mid-February, but the schedule is still hectic with eight games to play in January. Not that anyone is complaining. "As we enter the second half of the season we can take encouragement from the progress we've already made," states Gérard Houllier. "We've got ties in all the cups to look forward to while we're still well-placed to contest the top spots in the table." There's more good news with the arrival of Jari Litmanen from Barcelona. "I'm delighted," adds the boss. "We now have four top-quality forwards – vital for any club challenging for honours."

MONDAY 1/1/01
SOUTHAMPTON (H) **PREMIERSHIP**

SATURDAY 6/1/01
ROTHERHAM UNITED (H) **FA CUP 3R**

WEDNESDAY 10/1/01
CRYSTAL PALACE (A)
WORTHINGTON CUP SF 1L

SATURDAY 13/1/01
ASTON VILLA (A) **PREMIERSHIP**

SATURDAY 20/1/01
MIDDLESBROUGH (H) **PREMIERSHIP**

WEDNESDAY 24/1/01
CRYSTAL PALACE (H)
WORTHINGTON CUP SF 2L

SATURDAY 27/1/01
LEEDS UNITED (A) **FA CUP 4R**

WEDNESDAY 31/1/01
MANCHESTER CITY (A) **PREMIERSHIP**

LIVERPOOL 3 *Heskey 47 75 Hamann 73*
ROTHERHAM UNITED 0

LINE UP

1 WESTERVELD
2 HENCHOZ
12 HYYPIA
23 CARRAGHER
25 BISCAN
7 SMICER
13 MURPHY
16 HAMANN
21 McALLISTER
10 OWEN
8 HESKEY

SUBSTITUTES

26 NIELSEN
27 VIGNAL
Smicer 77
17 GERRARD
Owen 64
24 DIOMEDE
20 BARMBY
Heskey 81

BOOKED
BISCAN
SMICER

SENT OFF
BISCAN

1 GRAY
3 ARTELL
4 SCOTT
28 BRANSTON
5 GARNER
10 WARNE
12 TALBOT
14 WATSON
16 HURST
7 ROBINS
9 LEE

SUBSTITUTES

30 CONNOR
2 BEECH
20 MONKHOUSE
Warne 90
23 BERRY
Lee 90
24 SEDGWICK
Robins 70

BOOKED
TALBOT
WARNE
SCOTT

Igor Biscan protests his innocence to no avail

As Liverpool kicked off their attempt to win the FA Cup for the first time since 1992, Liverpudlian Ronnie Moore brought his second division Rotherham United to Anfield for what turned out to be a comfortable victory for the Reds.

Two Emile Heskey strikes and one from midfielder Dietmar Hamann finished off the brave Yorkshire side, whose 7,000 strong travelling support helped to create one of the best Anfield atmospheres of the season.

Rotherham boasted the best away form in their division and for much of the first half they matched Liverpool in midfield. There were a few early chances for the Reds, and defender Rob Scott made an excellent clearance off the line from Michael Owen.

Scott then almost made a mark at the other end, grazing the home crossbar to give Liverpool a scare. "I had to calm them down at half time because they were giddy about being level at Anfield," said Moore after the match.

The second half saw Houllier's men assert their superiority, with Emile Heskey heading goalwards from an Owen cross. A brief flicker of hope was provided for the Merry Millers when Igor Biscan was harshly dismissed for a second bookable offence. But the Reds raised their game with 10 men and Danny Murphy's dribble teed up Hamann for Liverpool's second before Emile Heskey unleashed a stunning third, blasting home a piledriver from over 20 yards.

Rotherham were left to rue a scoreline they felt flattered their more illustrious opponents, and to protest about Vladimir Smicer, whom they felt was diving.

"The way he went down was something we are not used to at our level." said Rod Scott.

Gérard Houllier saw it differently, but for the Reds, it was mission accomplished and a fifth-round trip to Leeds.

51

The number of successful passes made by midfielder Dietmar Hamann

Heskey double sees Liverpool through
Biscan sent off after second yellow card
Smicer embroiled in 'diving' dispute

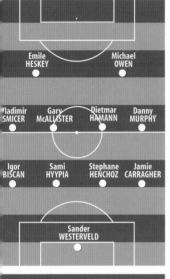

Emile **HESKEY**
Michael **OWEN**

ladimir **SMICER**
Gary **McALLISTER**
Dietmar **HAMANN**
Danny **MURPHY**

Igor **BISCAN**
Sami **HYYPIA**
Stephane **HENCHOZ**
Jamie **CARRAGHER**

Sander **WESTERVELD**

ERPOOL OFFICIAL MATCHDAY MAGAZINE
AN OF THE MATCH **VLADIMIR SMICER**

THOMMO'S VERDICT

"This was a highly professional performance from the lads. People were saying our results were flattering us at this point in the season, which was both out of order and ridiculous.

"To have a man sent off after a harsh decision and go on to win 3-0 is a very good display.

The players had to battle hard because Rotherham were a well-organised, powerful side.

"We limited them to one chance and if Michael Owen's effort had gone in early on, it could have killed the game off then. Our movement and passing were tremendous, particularly from

the likes of Danny Murphy and Vladimir Smicer. Emile Heskey also scored a couple of clinical goals.

"Obviously we were delighted to get through and be drawn against our old arch-rivals Leeds United at Elland Road, which was set up to be the tie of the fourth round."

Vladimir Smicer goes down to Rotherham's annoyance

CRYSTAL PALACE 2 *Rubins 55 Morrison 77*
LIVERPOOL 1 *Smicer 78*

LINE UP

35 KOLINKO
4 AUSTIN
33 HARRISON
5 ZHIYI
17 RUBINS
8 RODGER
2 SMITH
14 THOMSON
7 MULLINS
10 MORRISON
15 FORSSELL

SUBSTITUTES
21 GREGG
12 GRAY
18 CARLISLE
16 FRAMPTON
32 POLLOCK

1 WESTERVELD
6 BABBEL
2 HENCHOZ
12 HYYPIA
23 CARRAGHER
13 MURPHY
17 GERRARD
25 BISCAN
20 BARMBY
10 OWEN
8 HESKEY

SUBSTITUTES
26 NIELSEN
7 SMICER
  Murphy 63
21 McALLISTER
16 HAMANN
  Barmby 77
37 LITMANEN
  Owen 63

Jari Litmanen made
instant impact on his de…

Emile Heskey and Michael Owen squandered a host of chances on a dismal night at Selhurst Park as Clinton Morrison and Andrejs Rubins hit the target to give Palace a shock first-leg lead in the Worthington Cup semi.

Liverpool's troubles began as early as the 10th minute, when Heskey took Sami Hyypia's pass and muscled past Fan Zhiyi to cut back an inch-perfect pass to Michael Owen who somehow contrived to balloon it over the bar from eight yards out. Steven Gerrard then picked out Heskey with a through ball, but he blazed his shot over the bar.

The misses seemed to stir Alan Smith's men into life and on 26 minutes, Morrison, taking control of a ball from Mikael Forsell, unleashed a shot from the edge of the box that Sander Westerveld managed to tip over the bar. From the corner, Hyypia was forced to head off the line from Hayden Mullins before Dean Austin headed wide.

Palace continued to threaten after the break and broke the deadlock on 56 minutes, Latvian striker Rubins firing into the top corner.

Nick Barmby and Igor both came close but Palace doubled their lead on 77 minutes when Craig Harrison's cross from the left was cushioned down by Mikael Forsell and Morrison reacted quickest to power in th loose ball. The Eagles' joy was tempered just 90 seconds later, however, when new signing, Ja Litmanen, who had replaced Owen on 63 minutes, crossed from the right and Vladimir Smicer sidefooted home.

"Our finishing could have be better," said Gérard Houllier. "That was the only thing lacki from our game. The players created a lot o chances but when you away from home and you have between six and nine situations or one-on-ones, then you have to be two or thre goals up by half time."

72
The number of touches made by Liverpool's captain Sami Hyypia

- Palace take their chances to go 2-0 ahead
- A late goal from Vladi Smicer rescues Reds
- New signing Jari Litmanen makes his debut

Michael OWEN
Emile HESKEY

Igor BISCAN
Danny MURPHY
Steven GERRARD
Nick BARMBY

Jamie CARRAGHER
Sami HYYPIA
Stephane HENCHOZ
Markus BABBEL

Sander WESTERVELD

LIVERPOOL OFFICIAL MATCHDAY MAGAZINE
MAN OF THE MATCH STEVEN GERRARD

THOMMO'S VERDICT

"The cameras were at Selhurst Park for this one hoping for a slip-up on our part and I guess they got what they wanted to a certain extent.

"Being 2-0 down with 15 minutes to go was not what we had envisaged early on and it really was against the run of play. If we'd been 3-0 up at half time I don't think anyone could have complained. It was another example of our dominating the play but failing to finish teams off.

"We had so many one-on-one chances, while Palace rode their luck a bit and struck with their only two chances of the match. Vlad Smicer struck back with a good goal and so we went home with the tie still very much alive and looking forward to an exciting night up at Anfield infront of our own supporters.

"We knew if we took our chances we'd book ourselves a trip to the final in Cardiff in February."

Gerrard in the thick of the action in the middle of the park

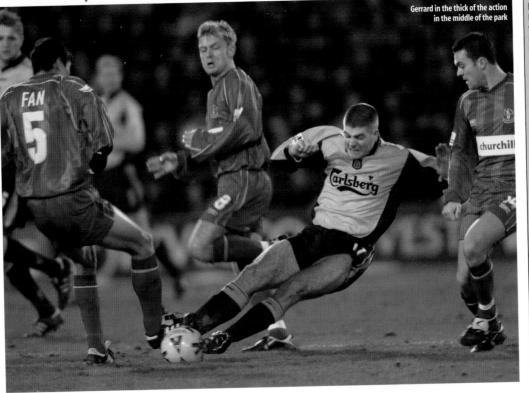

LIVERPOOL 5 *Smicer 12 Murphy 14 51 Biscan 18 Fowler 89*
CRYSTAL PALACE 0

LINE UP

1	WESTERVELD
17	GERRARD
2	HENCHOZ
12	HYYPIA
23	CARRAGHER
7	SMICER
21	McALLISTER
13	MURPHY
25	BISCAN
37	LITMANEN
9	FOWLER

SUBSTITUTES

26	NIELSEN
3	ZIEGE *Carragher 76*
16	HAMANN *Gerrard 68*
8	HESKEY
20	BARMBY *Smicer 70*

35	KOLINKO
2	SMITH
33	HARRISON
4	AUSTIN
14	THOMSON
18	CARLISLE
17	RUBINS
8	RODGER
11	BLACK
15	FORSSELL
10	MORRISON

SUBSTITUTES

6	RUDDOCK
32	POLLOCK *Carlisle 57*
27	KABBA
12	GRAY *Rubins 75*
21	GREGG *Forssell 83*

SENT OFF
KOLINKO

No quarter given: Pollock feels the full force of Hamann

- **Midfield hero Murphy at the double**
- **Biscan grabs his first goal for the Reds**
- **Fowler's late strike seals trip to Cardiff**

LIVERPOOL 5 *Smicer 12 Murphy 14 51 Biscan 18 Fowler 89*
CRYSTAL PALACE 0

Houllier's men atoned for their atrocious finishing in the first leg, brushing aside Crystal Palace to reach the Millennium Stadium and their first final in five years.

It was a night the manager and the fans won't forget in a hurry, and nor will Palace striker Clinton Morrison. After taunting Emile Heskey and Michael Owen for their poor performances at Selhurst Park, Morrison was the butt of the crowd's derision and to add insult to injury, hit an air shot in front of the Kop.

The tie was level after just 12 minutes. Vladimir Smicer raced on to a perfectly threaded pass from Robbie Fowler and beat Wayne Carlisle to drive his shot past Aleksandrs Kolinko.

Two minutes later, a beautiful cross from Jari Litmanen was brilliantly volleyed home by Danny Murphy from 15 yards. The third goal wasn't long in arriving, Fowler's intelligent backheel setting up Igor Biscan who galloped from halfway to steer his shot beyond Kolinko.

Gary McAllister nearly made it four when his thunderbolt hit the Palace upright and Litmanen generously headed a cross from Smicer into Fowler's path when it would have been easier to score himself.

Palace had a couple of chances, Tommy Black's free-kick testing Sander Westerveld. But six minutes after the break, Fowler's knockdown was picked up by Murphy who waltzed through to lift his shot over Kolinko for his second and Liverpool's fourth.

It finally fell apart for Alan Smith's men on 83 minutes when Fowler was hauled down by the Palace keeper who was promptly sent off. Fowler took his revenge six minutes later by sliding Murphy's pass under the body of substitute Matthew Gregg.

Vladimir Smicer celebrates Liverpool's opener with a little help from Igor Biscan and Robbie Fowler

75
The percentage of Danny Murphy's passes that reached a team-mate

"Houllier's pre-season prophecy that silverware would return after a six-year famine is now just 90 minutes away from being fulfilled"

Paul Joyce *Daily Express*

Star man Danny Murphy clips home the fourth for Liverpool

DO THEY MEAN US

"I want to give all the credit to Liverpool because they played really well tonight. They're exceptional – strong and powerful – and were simply too good for us. I wish them luck in the final. I felt Robbie Fowler would have an influence, he is of this city and wanted to set the place ablaze"
Palace manager, Alan Smith

The Daily Telegraph
sport
Football: Worthington Cup
Fowler has the final word for Liverpool

"Gérard Houllier's pre-season prophecy that silverware would return to Anfield following a six-year famine is now just 90 minutes away from being fulfilled. His players did not so much knock on the door to a final appearance as hammer it down"
Paul Joyce *Daily Express*

"It was Merseyside's night. The Kop roared its affection for Houllier, which the Frenchman acknowledged with a diffident wave. He has risen to stern tests and Palace were brushed aside in a manner that recalled Liverpool in the 80s"
Tim Rich
The Independent

Robbie **FOWLER** Jari **LITMANEN**

Igor **BISCAN** Danny **MURPHY** Gary **McALLISTER** Vladimir **SMICER**

Jamie **CARRAGHER** Sami **HYYPIA** Stephane **HENCHOZ** Steven **GERRARD**

Sander **WESTERVELD**

THOMMO'S VERDICT

"Sometimes you just get a gut feeling it's going to be your night, and that was evident in the dressing room before this game. We were determined to make amends after a disappointing result at Selhurst Park. The attitude from every one of the players was right, and straight from the whistle

I sensed we would win it.

"What can you say about this performance? It was the way this club should play. You can't do it all the time, obviously, but everything just seemed to click for this match.

"We passed and moved fantastically and the finishing was first-class. The

atmosphere was absolutely electric, both sets of fans played their part, and the Kop was tremendous, just like a European night.

"The only player I'll single out from this game is Danny Murphy. He was awesome in midfield and gave everything from start to finish. He's really come on this season."

LEEDS UNITED 0
LIVERPOOL 2 *Barmby 87 Heskey 90*

1 MARTYN
2 KELLY
3 HARTE
6 WOODGATE
29 FERDINAND
11 BOWYER
19 BAKKE
23 BATTY
21 MATTEO
7 KEANE
9 VIDUKA

SUBSTITUTES
13 ROBINSON
18 MILLS
4 DACOURT
16 WILCOX
17 SMITH
Keane72

BOOKED
HARTE

1 WESTERVELD
6 BABBEL
2 HENCHOZ
12 HYYPIA
23 CARRAGHER
13 MURPHY
16 HAMANN
21 McALLISTER
25 BISCAN
7 SMICER
9 FOWLER

SUBSTITUTES
26 NIELSEN
3 ZIEGE
Murphy 75
20 BARMBY
Babbel 67
8 HESKEY
Smicer 72
37 LITMANEN

BOOKED
MCALLISTER
SMICER
BISCAN
ZIEGE

Danger for Liverpool as Westerveld jumps for a cross

It was the second time Liverpool travelled to Elland Road in the season and they had revenge in mind. They had lost an extraordinary game two months earlier 4-3, after being 2-0 up, and they met this time in the glamour tie of the fourth round.

It looked like another thrilling encounter was on the cards when Robbie Keane almost put Leeds in front after 35 seconds, but Stephane Henchoz cleared brilliantly off the line to prevent a nightmare start for the Reds. The rest of the game failed to live up to its explosive opening, however, and it was scrappy and aggressive in parts. On 37 minutes Leeds' Lee Bowyer slammed Gary McAllister in the face with his elbow, an incident that went unpunished.

"It upset me because it happened right in front of me," said an unhappy Gérard Houllier after the match. "He should have got at least a booking for it."

Leeds were again prevented from taking the lead in the second half, when Sami Hyypia cleared off the line from Norwegian, Erik Bakke's shot.

With neither side able to capitalise on their periods of pressure it looked certain the game was heading for a rematch at Anfield, until an inspirational flash of skill was delivered by Robbie Fowler, who'd been influential throughout. With two minutes on the clock, his powerful shot rebounded off the post, to be met by sub Nick Barmby, who lashed it into the roof of the net. Two minutes later the Reds sealed their place in the fifth round when a skilful Fowler dribble and cross set up Emile Heskey to power home a 72 mph screamer.

"The difference was, Liverpool took their chances," said Leeds boss David O'Leary. His Anfield opposite was delighted. "Robbie did marvellously well," said Houllier. "This club is about winning trophies."

41
The number of successful passes made by midfielder Didi Hamann

■ **Revenge is sweet as Reds launch late show**
■ **Bowyer challenge leaves Houllier fuming**
■ **Inspirational Fowler leads from the front**

Robbie
FOWLER

Vladimir
SMICER

Igor
BISCAN

Gary
McALLISTER

Dietmar
HAMANN

Danny
MURPHY

Jamie
CARRAGHER

Sami
HYYPIA

Stephane
HENCHOZ

Marcus
BABBEL

Sander
WESTERVELD

LIVERPOOL OFFICIAL MATCHDAY MAGAZINE
MAN OF THE MATCH ROBBIE FOWLER

THOMMO'S VERDICT

"Before kick-off, this game had been billed as the the tie of the round but to be honest it never really lived up to expectations. The first half was pretty sloppy and we rode our luck a fair bit. In the second half, we made some tactical changes, we played a lot better and although we didn't make a breakthrough until the very end we never really felt we were in danger.

"As the game wore on you could tell that Leeds would be happy with a draw but that was the last thing we wanted as our fixtures were already starting to pile up. Gérard has said all along that substitutions are crucial these days and he was proved correct again at Elland Road.

"The three lads we brought on – Christian Ziege, Nick Barmby and Emile Heskey – all played their part in the win. They were good goals and Robbie Fowler was heavily involved in our best moves. A fantastic result."

DO THEY MEAN US?

"O'Leary's team was expected to offer a threat to the dominance of United this season. But it is a resurgent Liverpool who have ensured they will be the team who start next season as the most credible challengers to the Old Trafford trophy machine"
Ian Edwards *The Mirror*

Leeds sunk by subs

"Fowler was the root of both goals against Leeds and looked every inch the England striker in the waiting"
Joe Lovejoy
The Sunday Times

"I still have a lot of time for Liverpool. I've got two season tickets and when I get the chance I go and see them. Robbie Fowler and I started at the same time and we're still pals. He's the best finisher I've ever seen"
Leeds' Dominic Matteo

"Houllier's done a wonderful job since taking charge. The progress he speaks of has indeed been made, the fact they're the only Premiership club to remain in three cup competitions is testament to that"
Matt Lawton
The Telegraph

Back in midfield, Robbie tangles with David Batty

Emile Heskey and co lead
Aston Villa a merry dance

That's the trouble with cup campaigns. No sooner do you get a breather in one than another one comes along to take its place. Despite the suspension of Uefa Cup duty until February, the Reds now have the FA Cup as well as the Worthington Cup to fit around their Premiership commitments.

They remain unbeaten in the League, however, leaving it late to beat Southampton on New Year's Day but spanking Aston Villa on their own ground in arguably their best away performance to date. A week later, though, there's frustration at home to Middlesbrough, whom new boss Terry Venables guides to a goalless draw, and at Maine Road where relegation-battling Manchester City come from behind to grab a point.

Liverpool still move up to fourth in the table, three points behind second-placed Sunderland and one behind Arsenal with a game in hand on both. Ipswich, too, are on 40 points, but their goal difference is inferior to the Reds.

FA CARLING PREMIERSHIP

MONDAY 1/1/01
LIVERPOOL 2 Gerrard 12, Babbel 86
SOUTHAMPTON 1 Soltvedt 20

SATURDAY 13/1/01
ASTON VILLA 0
LIVERPOOL 3 Murphy 24 53, Gerrard 32

SATURDAY 20/1/01
LIVERPOOL 0
MIDDLESBROUGH 0

WEDNESDAY 31/1/01
MANCHESTER CITY 1 Tiatto 47
LIVERPOOL 1 Heskey 44

MONDAY 1/1/01 TO WEDNESDAY 31/1/01

THE UNDEFEATED

ENTER THE
GLADIATORS

A pre-match fag was part of the
ritual at the Stadio Olimpico

If it's Thursday, it must be Roma. And if it's Sunday, take your pick from the last 16 of the FA Cup and the Worthington Cup final. Destiny beckons for Gérard Houllier's treble-chasers. But first there are two consecutive Saturdays in the Premiership. The game at Sunderland is a Champions League six-pointer and a tough test before the Reds jet off to Italy for the first leg of a titanic tie that Roma boss Fabio Capello has dubbed, "The one we didn't want to play." He rates the Reds as the strongest side left in the tournament and claims, "If we're going to progress any further we'll have to be at our very best."

For Liverpool, the worst-case scenario is that, within 10 days, they could be out of all three cup competitions. "We've achieved nothing yet," warns the boss. "It may be a footballing cliche to say we're taking each game as it comes but that's the only way to remain completely focused on the task in hand." There's a timely boost, though, as Gary McAllister signs a new deal keeping him at Anfield for another season.

SATURDAY 3/2/01
WEST HAM UNITED (H) **PREMIERSHIP**

SATURDAY 10/2/01
SUNDERLAND (A) **PREMIERSHIP**

THURSDAY 15/2/01
ROMA (A) **UEFA CUP 4R 1L**

SUNDAY 18/2/01
MANCHESTER CITY (H) **FA CUP 5R**

THURSDAY 22/2/01
ROMA (H) **UEFA CUP 4R 2L**

SUNDAY 25/2/01
BIRMINGHAM CITY (CARDIFF) **WC FINAL**

ROMA 0
LIVERPOOL 2 *Owen 46 71*

1 ANTONIOLI
2 CAFU
19 SAMUEL
23 RINALDI
28 MANGONE
8 NAKATA
11 EMERSON
17 TOMMASI
32 CANDELA
9 MONTELLA
24 DELVECCHIO

SUBSTITUTES
22 LUPATELLI
7 DI FRANCESCO
5 ASSUNÇAO
   Nakata 50
25 GUIGOU
   Delvecchio 82
16 D'AGOSTINO
18 BATISTUTA
   Tommasi 66
21 BALBO

BOOKED
MANGONE

1 WESTERVELD
6 BABBEL
2 HENCHOZ
12 HYYPIA
23 CARRAGHER
20 BARMBY
16 HAMANN
21 McALLISTER
3 ZIEGE
9 FOWLER
10 OWEN

SUBSTITUTES
19 ARPHEXAD
27 VIGNAL
29 WRIGHT
33 NAVARRO
24 DIOMEDE
7 SMICER
   Ziege 74
37 LITMANEN
   Owen 79

Just 45 seconds after the restart, Owen pounces

It may have been only the first leg of a fourth-round Uefa Cup tie, but history ensured that Liverpool against Roma at the Olympic Stadium could never be just another match.

The Reds returned to the scene of two European Cup triumphs, to face opponents they had beaten in a breathtaking penalty shoot-out in 1984, and the talk was of revenge for Roma and Liverpool's sternest test for many years. The manner in which they rose to the occasion means the game will be remembered as one of the finest displays ever by an English team away from home.

Michael Owen struck twice, his first goals of the year, to beat a Roma side undefeated at home all season and running away with Serie A. At the other end, heroic defending from a settled backline muted some of the world's best attacking talent, as Delvecchio, Montella and Batistuta were all effectively shackled.

The first half was fitful for the Reds, with Stephane Henchoz and Sami Hyypia having to be at their best to contain the Roma forwards. But for all their pressure, the home side created few clear-cut opportunities, the best being a near-post header from Delvecchio that flashed wide.

Just after the interval, a moment of madness presented Michael

46
The number of times goalkeeper Sander Westerveld touched the ball

Owen with his opener. Rinaldi's wayward pass was intercepted by the striker, who drove his shot into the net low past Antonioli to stun the home crowd.

The Italian side found it hard to lift themselves and the Reds began to dominate. In the 71st minute, Owen headed home Ziege's low cross, sending the travelling fans into delirious chants of "We always win in Rome".

A proud Gérard Houllier expressed his delight after the match. "To come to the home of the Serie A leaders and win so convincingly is wonderful," he said. "But we musn't get carried away."

- Owen double stuns Serie A pacesetters
- Hyypia and Henchoz dominant at the back
- Hamann imperious in Reds engine room

Robbie **FOWLER**

Michael **OWEN**

Christian **ZIEGE**

Gary **McALLISTER**

Dietmar **HAMANN**

Nick **BARMBY**

Jamie **CARRAGHER**

Sami **HYYPIA**

Stephane **HENCHOZ**

Markus **BABBEL**

Sander **WESTERVELD**

LIVERPOOL OFFICIAL MATCHDAY MAGAZINE
MAN OF THE MATCH **DIETMAR HAMANN**

THOMMO'S VERDICT

"We were ecstatic with this result. It was one of the best performances any Liverpool side has ever put in on foreign soil. But the job was only half done so we knew we'd have to concentrate for the home leg.

"It was a brilliant team performance, from the goalkeeper forward. Sander Westerveld gave us confidence with his handling, while the defence was extremely solid all night, with Stephane Henchoz and Sami Hyypia dominating, and Didi Hamann gave the complete performance in midfield, competing for every ball and passing brilliantly.

"We stood strong for the opening 20 minutes, which were crucial, and after scoring early in the second half we started to gain in confidence and got our passing going.

"It was fantastic to see Michael Owen back to his best and the goals were a just reward for a tremendous performance. Every player did Liverpool proud."

DO THEY MEAN US?

"The ghosts of Liverpool teams past walked again in the Olympic stadium last night. Twice crowned European champions here in Rome, two goals here by Owen brought a revived Liverpool side an unexpectedly handsome cushion for the return leg. Shankly and Paisley would have been proud of Liverpool's resilience"
Andrew Longmore
The Independent

"Nothing should detract from Liverpool's sweet victory nor detract their sense of satisfaction. They played with intelligence and style, defended with gusto and bravery and, after negotiating an uncomfortable early spell, they never once looked like losing"
Ian Ross
The Guardian

The Guardian
Sport

Owen thrives on Roma therapy

"The score is very sad for us. We gave a gift to Liverpool. They made it difficult for us. We made a good start but Liverpool made it difficult. I'd have preferred to have given Batistuta more time but it is difficult for him to play three games in eight days"
Fabio Capello

Hamann was first to the ball all night

LIVERPOOL 4 Litmanen 6 pen Heskey 12 Smicer 52 pen Babbel 83
MANCHESTER CITY 2 Kanchelskis 28 Goater 88

LINE UP

1 WESTERVELD
6 BABBEL
2 HENCHOZ
12 HYYPIA
23 CARRAGHER
7 SMICER
16 HAMANN
25 BISCAN
3 ZIEGE
8 HESKEY
37 LITMANEN

SUBSTITUTES
19 ARPHEXAD
27 VIGNAL
20 BARMBY
  Litmanen 45
9 FOWLER
  Heskey 83
10 OWEN
  Smicer 76

1 WEAVER
22 DUNNE
5 MORRISON
7 PRIOR
36 GRANVILLE
12 KANCHELSKIS
4 WIEKENS
15 HAALAND
19 TIATTO
10 GOATER
21 HUCKERBY

SUBSTITUTES
26 McKINNEY
28 GRANT
  Morrison 59
14 TAYLOR
3 EDGHILL
29 WRIGHT-PHILLIPS

BOOKED
HAALAND

Goalscorer Emile Heskey rampages through Manchester City's defence

It was just three days after the glories of Rome, but Liverpool displayed plenty of resilience to keep their cup treble bid alive with a 4-2 destruction of struggling Manchester City.

Having started with Michael Owen and Robbie Fowler upfront in Italy, Houllier brought in his other pair of star strikers. Emile Heskey was again devastating and Jari Litmanen impressed with a mesmerising first-half performance, striking home a penalty and giving a masterclass in passing, movement and vision before leaving the field injured early in the second half.

The Reds' first goal came from the spot after Vladimir Smicer was brought down in the box by City keeper Nicky Weaver just six minutes into the game. It was a controversial moment, as referee Graham Poll lost his footing while awarding the foul.

"It was a ridiculous decision," blasted City boss Joe Royle.

Litmanen was instrumental in the second goal, too, when he played an irresistible curling pass into the path of Heskey, who lashed the ball past Weaver from the edge of the box for his 18th strike of the season.

As Liverpool fans contemplated a thrashing, Andrei Kanchelskis made it 2-1, powering home a deflected shot following a corner.

But after the restart, Liverpool increased the tempo and carved out a number of chances, restoring the two-goal lead when the City keeper again chopped down the marauding Smicer, who this time converted the spot-kick himself.

The game was put beyond City when Markus Babbel neatly headed home Christian Ziege's free-kick, and despite a late Shaun Goater consolation strike, the Reds held on for victory.

6
The number of Liverpool shots on goal blocked by City players

- Litmanen puts on a virtuoso display
- Smicer causes havoc in City defence
- Heskey and Babbel complete the rout

Jari LITMANEN Emile HESKEY

Christian ZIEGE Igor BISCAN Dietmar HAMANN Vladimir SMICER

Jamie CARRAGHER Sami HYYPIA Stephane HENCHOZ Markus BABBEL

Sander WESTERVELD

LIVERPOOL OFFICIAL MATCHDAY MAGAZINE
MAN OF THE MATCH **VLADIMIR SMICER**

THOMMO'S VERDICT

"The lads deserved enormous credit for the football they produced in this match, coming straight from our victory in Rome. We imposed ourselves on a physical game against a team who weren't going to lie down despite their lowly position in the League table, and Joe Royle's teams will always give you a battle. But we still managed to play our passing game and we got a couple of goals on the board early on.

"Jari Litmanen had a great influence in the first 45 minutes and Vladimir Smicer was on song all afternoon, causing the City defence plenty of problems with his running. We were disappointed to let them back into it with a sloppy goal from Kanchelskis when it looked like we could have run away with it, but fortunately Smicer won us another penalty, and a great header from Markus Babbel saw us home. All in all it was a magnificent performance, and all eyes were then on Prenton Park."

Vladimir Smicer earns the first of two spot-kicks after just six minutes

LIVERPOOL 0
ROMA 1 *Guigou 70*

LINE UP

1 WESTERVELD
6 BABBEL
2 HENCHOZ
12 HYYPIA
23 CARRAGHER
16 HAMANN
20 BARMBY
21 McALLISTER
3 ZIEGE
8 HESKEY
10 OWEN

SUBSTITUTES
19 ARPHEXAD
27 VIGNAL
29 WRIGHT
24 DIOMEDE
7 SMICER
   Owen 67
9 FOWLER
   Barmby 81
37 LITMANEN

1 ANTONIOLI
15 ZEBINA
19 SAMUEL
3 ZAGO
23 RINALDI
17 TOMMASI
5 ASSUNÇAO
32 CANDELA
8 NAKATA
9 MONTELLA
24 DELVECCHIO

SUBSTITUTES
22 LUPATELLI
30 BOVO
7 DI FRANCESCO
25 GUIGOU
   Rinaldi 59
16 D'AGOSTINO
18 BATISTUTA
   Delvecchio 59
21 BALBO
   Montella 79

BOOKED
MONTELLA,
ASSUNÇAO , ZEBINA
SAMUEL , GUIGOU
TOMMASI, CANDELA

SENT OFF
TOMMASI

Vincent Candela hauls down Owen to give Liverpool a first-half penalty

- **Reds march on after night of high drama**
- **Kop in full voice in tribute to Bob Paisley**
- **Owen misses penalty as tempers flare**

LIVERPOOL 0
ROMA 1 *Guigou 70*

A night earmarked as a celebration of the achievements of Bob Paisley, this was always likely to be special. It was and despite controversy and a dangerously close finish, the result and atmosphere ensured it was an evening to remember for the Anfield crowd.

Both sides had chances to swing the game their way, but for all the passion and pressure of the first half, few chances were actually created. A Sami Hyypia header was saved off the line, and Michael Owen latched on to a shoddy back pass from

Nakata, but sent his shot wide.

On the hour Owen had another chance to kill the game when Jonathan Zebina impeded Emile Heskey in the box, but his penalty attempt was gathered by the keeper. Ten minutes later Roma took control as a powerful 25-yard strike from Gianni Guigou beat Sander Westerveld to ensure a tense finish.

The game was thrown into controversy soon after, when Babbel appeared to handball in the box. The referee pointed to the penalty spot, before changing his mind and despite Italian protestations, the spot kick was

not given. As Roma continued to press forward looking for the equaliser, tempers frayed and Tomassi was dismissed for a second offence.

In the end, Roma failed to capitalise on all their late pressure and a resilient Liverpool defence held on, kept their discipline and overcame their sternest test of the cup so far to win 2-1 on aggregate.

"Putting Roma out is a huge achievement," said Gérard Houllier. "They are one of the best teams in Europe. They were better than us, but our defence was superb."

A night to remember: the Kop in full voice in tribute to Bob Paisley

79
The percentage of successful passes by Stephane Henchoz, Liverpool's highest

'Putting Roma out is a huge achievement, they are one of the best teams in Europe. They were better than us but our defence was superb"
Gérard Houllier

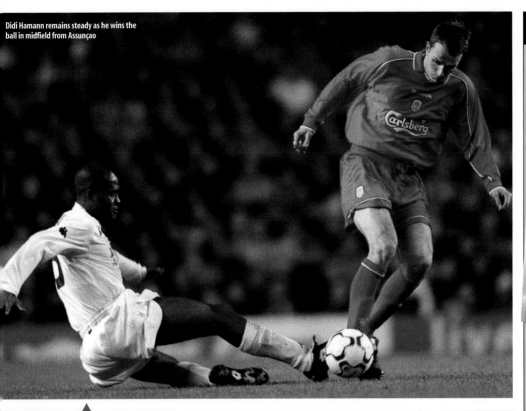

Didi Hamann remains steady as he wins the ball in midfield from Assunçao

DO THEY MEAN US?

"On the night, the glory – and a burning sense of injustice – went to Fabio Capello's side, but it is Gérard Houllier's team who will now meet Porto in the quarter-finals of a European adventure fast developing beyond his wildest dreams"
Paul Joyce *The Express*

"At the end of a thoroughly nerve-wracking night, Fabio Capello's fine Italian side were put out of the Uefa Cup by Liverpool but Gérard Houllier's men took a physical and mental battering on the way… This was a test of Liverpool's character but they held on and now face Porto in the quarter-finals"
Henry Winter
The Daily Telegraph

"It was close, at times almost unbearably so. Whatever the rights and wrongs, this was another battle won by a team that is acquiring an indomitable spirit in a quest for success in three cup competitions"
Oliver Kay *The Times*

LIVERPOOL OFFICIAL MATCHDAY MAGAZINE
MAN OF THE MATCH **DIETMAR HAMANN**

Emile **HESKEY**   Michael **OWEN**

Christian **ZIEGE**   Gary **McALLISTER**   Dietmar **HAMANN**   Nick **BARMBY**

Jamie **CARRAGHER**   Sami **HYYPIA**   Stephane **HENCHOZ**   Markus **BABBEL**

Sander **WESTERVELD**

THOMMO'S VERDICT

"We'd hurt the pride of one of the best teams in Europe in the first leg, beating them on their own ground, and in the return, they produced a top-class performance at Anfield but we held on to come out of it as winners.

"They've got some superb, world-class players and they knocked the ball around nicely but in the end they didn't really cause Sander Westerveld too many problems.

"I'm not saying it was easy though, and it was a nerve-wracking finale but that's when the crowd came into their own and played their part. They were absolutely brilliant, and were in outstanding voice for Bob Paisley night. They really lifted us up near the end when we needed it most.

"Didi Hamann was again the star in midfield and he put in a tremendous all-round display just as he had in Rome a week earlier."

LIVERPOOL 1 *Fowler 30 Liverpool win 5-4 on penalties after extra time*
BIRMINGHAM CITY 1 *Purse 90 pen*

LINE UP

1 WESTERVELD
6 BABBEL
2 HENCHOZ
12 HYYPIA
23 CARRAGHER
17 GERRARD
16 HAMANN
25 BISCAN
7 SMICER
9 FOWLER
8 HESKEY

SUBSTITUTES
19 ARPHEXAD
3 ZIEGE
Biscan 96
20 BARMBY
Smicer 83
21 McALLISTER
Gerrard 76
10 OWEN

BOOKED
HENCHOZ
HAMANN

1 BENNETT
2 EADEN
3 GRAINGER
5 PURSE
17 M JOHNSON
7 McCARTHY
32 SONNER
12 O'CONNOR
11 LAZARIDIS
9 HORSFIELD
24 ADEBOLA

SUBSTITUTES
13 POOLE
10 HUGHES
Sonner 70
8 MARCELO
Horsfield 80
19 A JOHNSON
Adebola 46
6 HOLDSWORTH

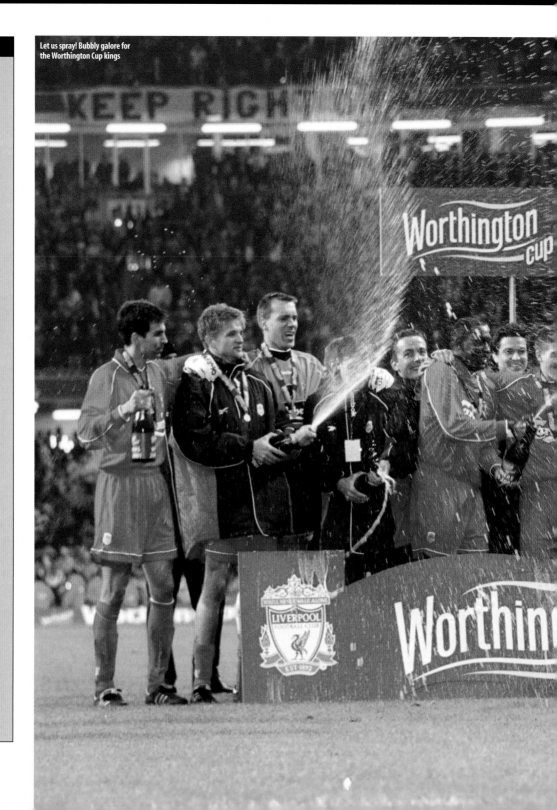

Let us spray! Bubbly galore for the Worthington Cup kings

- **Reds first to win League Cup outside England**
- **Plucky Blues force extra time with late penalty**
- **Robbie's first-half rocket thrills watching millions**

LIVERPOOL 1 *Fowler 29 Liverpool win 5-4 on penalties after extra time*
BIRMINGHAM CITY 1 *Purse 93 pen*

Silverware at last! Robbie Fowler lifted Liverpool's first trophy for six years at the end of an epic struggle in Cardiff. And he scored an unforgettable goal that looked to have won it until Birmingham's braves snatched a last-gasp equaliser that meant extra time and penalties.

The breakthrough came in the 29th minute. Sander Westerveld's long clearance was headed on by Emile Heskey and the ball bounced once before Fowler spotted Ian Bennett outside his six-yard box and looped a sublime volley over the keeper's despairing dive.

The balance, however, began to tip after the interval. Steven Gerrard went off with cramp and the West Midlanders started to show the form that had seen off high-flying Ipswich in the semi.

But they were tying red ribbons to the cup when Stephane Henchoz felled Martin O'Connor in the box in the third minute of stoppage time and Darren Purse fired a nerveless penalty to force extra time.

Two hours couldn't separate the teams and it was down to penalties, the first shoot-out in a major English cup final. Gary McAllister sidefooted Liverpool's

first home, but Westerveld guessed when Martin Grainger was going to put it and saved to his left. Birmingham regained parity however when Bennett stopped Didi Hamann's blast. At 4-4 it was into sudden death. Jamie Carragher stroked past Bennett, and Westerveld dived to his left to stop the unfortunate Andy Johnson's weak effort.

"It's nice because people were belittling the competition," said a joyous Fowler afterwards. "We'd set out to win it from the start and hopefully it's the stepping stone for us to go on and win more medals and trophies."

The best goal scored in a cup final? For sheer audacity, it's got to be right up there

18
The number of headed clearances by the mighty Finn Sami Hyypia

"We'd set out to win this cup from the very start and hopefully it's the stepping stone for us to go on and win more medals and trophies"

Robbie Fowler

OPTA'S PLAYER BY PLAYER WORTHINGTON CUP FINAL STATS

	Gary McALLISTER	Nick BARMBY	Emile HESKEY	Sander WESTERVELD	Stephane HENCHOZ	Vladimir SMICER	Robbie FOWLER	Sami HYYPIA	Dietmar HAMANN	Jamie CARRAGHER	Steven GERRARD	Christian ZIEGE	Markus BABBEL	Igor BISCAN	TOTAL
TIME ON PITCH	42	37	120	120	120	83	120	120	120	120	78	24	120	96	1320
SHOTS															
GOAL SCORED							1								1
SHOT ON TARGET	1					2	2	1							6
SHOT OFF TARGET						1	4	1						1	7
BLOCKED SHOT			1			2	3				1				7
HIT THE WOODWORK									1						1
OWN GOAL															0
PASSES															
PASS TO OWN PLAYER	11	12	29	8	25	14	23	44	62	36	25	7	29	30	355
PASS TO OPPOSITION	4	1	12	9	10	10	12	16	5	20	14	4	13	10	140
PASS TO SCORING ZONE (OWN PLAYER)	1				1	2					1		1		6
PASS TO SCORING ZONE (OPPOSITION)		1	1			4					5	1	3	2	17
GOAL ASSIST			1												1
PASS COMPLETION	75%	86%	70%	47%	72%	53%	66%	73%	93%	64%	58%	58%	65%	71%	70%
DRIBBLES and RUNS															
POSSESSION RETAINED		2	1			2	1	2	5	1	2	1	2	5	24
POSSESSION LOST			3			3	6		1		2		2	1	18
CONTROLLED FIRST TOUCH															0
DRIBBLE SUCCESS	0%	100%	25%	0%	0%	40%	14%	100%	83%	100%	50%	100%	50%	83%	57%
FOULS and FREE KICKS															
FREE-KICK – FOUL			3		3	2	1	1	4	1			2	4	21
FREE-KICK – HANDBALL															0
PENALTY CONCEDED					1										1
FREE-KICK – OFFSIDE			3						1		1				5
YELLOW CARDS					1				1						2
RED CARDS															0
TACKLES															
TACKLES ATTEMPTED	4	0	0	0	7	4	2	7	3	7	3	0	4	3	43
TACKLE WON	2				6	3	1	6	3	7	2		4	2	36
TACKLE LOST	2				1	1	1	1						1	7
TACKLE SUCCESS RATE	50%	0%	0%	0%	86%	75%	50%	86%	100%	100%	100%	0%	100%	67%	84%
TOTAL TIMES TACKLED	2	0	7	0	0	5	9	3	3	0	3	0	4	2	38
TACKLED, RETAINED POSSESSION	1		1			1	5	1	1				1	1	12
TACKLED, LOST POSSESSION	1		6			4	4	2	2		3		3	1	26
POSSESSION RETENTION RATE	50%	0%	14%	0%	0%	20%	56%	33%	33%	0%	0%	0%	25%	50%	32%
CLEARANCES, BLOCKS, INTERCEPTIONS															
HEADED CLEARANCES			1		8			18	3	7			5	1	43
OTHER CLEARANCES				1	4			4	1	2			1	1	14
INTERCEPTIONS									1				1		2
CLEARANCES OFF THE GOAL LINE															0
BLOCKED SHOTS					2	1							1		4
BLOCKED CROSS					4	1			1				2		09
TOTAL TOUCHES	21	16	49	51	61	45	55	93	83	73	53	13	64	54	731

SANDER'S STATS

GOALS CONCEDED	
SHOTS FROM INSIDE BOX	
SHOTS FROM OUTSIDE BOX	
SHOTS FROM SET PIECE	
SHOTS FROM PENALTY	1
ERROR LEADING TO GOAL	
CLEAN SHEET	
SAVES	
SHOTS FROM INSIDE BOX	1
SHOTS FROM OUTSIDE BOX	2
SHOTS FROM SET PIECE	
SHOTS FROM PENALTY	
SMOTHERING THE BALL	
SAVES TO SHOTS RATIO	75%
THROWS	
TOTAL	5
TO OWN PLAYER	5
TO OPPOSITION PLAYER	
THROW COMPLETION RATE	100%
KICKING FROM HANDS and GOAL KICKS	
TOTAL	20
TO OWN PLAYER	7
TO OPPOSITION PLAYER	13
KICKING COMPLETION RATE	35%
KICKING IN OPEN PLAY	
TOTAL	17
TO OWN PLAYER	8
TO OPPOSITION PLATER	9
OPEN PLAY COMPLETION RATE	47%
CATCHING and PUNCHING	
CATCHES	3
PUNCHES	2
BALLS DROPPED	
CROSSES NOT CLAIMED	
CATCH SUCCESS RATE	100%

"WHAT A FINISH!" Alan Parry and Brain Marwood, Sky Sports

AP Fowler! Produces an absolutely magnificent goal to give the Premiership club the lead! What a finish by Robbie Fowler! He really turned back the clock with that goal! **BM** If anybody had any doubts about his sharpness, look at this. Top-drawer finishing. A magnificent strike for a player perfectly in form. **AP** Fowler's sixth goal in the competition this season. Liverpool have the breakthrough.

LIVERPOOL 1 *Fowler 29 Liverpool win 5-4 on penalties after extra time*
BIRMINGHAM CITY 1 *Purse 93 pen*

BIRMINGHAM PENALTY 6
TAKER ANDY JOHNSON
AIM BOTTOM RIGHT
Sudden death, and the pressure is on Birmingham's youngster to emulate Jamie Carragher's cool kick. In front of the Liverpool fans, his shot is firm and well-placed but not enough to beat Sander Westerveld.

DUTCH COURAGE

Ticker pounding crazily against your chest wall? Nerves so tense you could ride a unicycle over them? Good job Sander was in goal, then. "I'm sure most of our supporters were really nervous," said the hero of the hour. "But I can honestly say I wasn't. I've never lost a penalty shoot-out in my life. In Holland I had a reputation for being a good penalty-stopper, but because a couple of players had scored against me since I've been at Liverpool,

the lads had asked me jokingly if I'd ever saved one. Well, now they know. Saving the first kick gave me a great feeling. Birmingham seemed to favour putting their kicks to my left, and on the last penalty that's where I decided to dive. I saw the ball coming towards me, but it took ages because of what was going through my mind. I got goose pimples when I was flying through the air and when I kept the shot out it was the best feeling in the world."

> **"The last kick seemed to take ages but I got goose pimples when I dived and when I kept it out it was the best feeling in the world"**
>
> Sander Westerveld

"Sorry, old bean, I don't speak fluent Brummie"

DO THEY MEAN US?

MondaySport Footba

Liverpool late show is just the beginning

"The key in the door of the Anfield silverware cabinet had not turned for six years until yesterday. But Gérard Houllier has rescued Liverpool from potentially terminal decline with what could be the first of many great cup triumphs"
Paul Hayward *The Daily Telegraph*

"Mr Houllier told us we were good enough to be in the Premiership. He shook everybody by the hand and offered his sincere condolences for the way we were forced to submit to defeat. He didn't need to say that. It was the gesture of a genuine and generous football man"
Birmingham's no11, Stan Lazaridis

"Fowler's beautifully struck goal, along with the industry and intelligence of his all-round performance can hardly have failed to impress Sven Goran Eriksson"
David Lacey *The Guardian*

"Every long march begins with a single step and Liverpool will hope that a record sixth League Cup win could prove a decisive moment in their 21st-century history"
Martin Lipton *Daily Mail*

LIVERPOOL OFFICIAL MATCHDAY MAGAZINE
MAN OF THE MATCH SAMI HYYPIA

Emile **HESKEY**   Robbie **FOWLER**

Vladimir **SMICER**   Igor **BISCAN**   Dietmar **HAMANN**   Steven **GERRARD**

Jamie **CARRAGHER**   Sami **HYYPIA**   Stephane **HENCHOZ**   Markus **BABBEL**

Sander **WESTERVELD**

THOMMO'S VERDICT

"It was a magnificent occasion, with a superb stadium really fit to host a final. To be fair, Cardiff's Millennium Stadium was as good if not better than Wembley in terms of the atmosphere.

"Birmingham City were hard opponents – we knew from the start they'd give it everything – but really we should have killed the game off early. It was a great start for us and Robbie's goal was wonderful. Only he could score a goal like that on such a big occasion.

"He played well all day, as did Didi Hamann in midfield and all the lads in defence. But we tired a little towards the end, they got their chance in the very last minute and we ended up with penalties after extra time.

"Even so, we were always confident we'd win on the spot kicks and the lads held their nerve. It's fantastic for us to get our first trophy in the bag so early on."

No fear: Jari sends Sorensen the wrong way to prise a point away from Wearside

Four Premiership points from a possible six is a good return for a Reds side about to enter the most important fortnight of the season so far. An easy 3-0 win at home to West Ham United – notable for the League debuts of Grégory Vignal and Stephen Wright – is followed by a massive game at Sunderland.

Roared on by over 47,000 fans, the Black Cats take the lead through Liverpool old boy Don Hutchison and threaten to score again until Gary McAllister is tripped in the box with 11 minutes remaining and Jari Litmanen coolly converts the penalty.

Robbie Fowler has a late winner disallowed, but Gérard Houllier is more than happy with a steely performance that puts Liverpool third. "We knew it would be a battle," he says. "But we showed we can stick together as a team." The stats show the defence is back to its watertight best: just five goals have been conceded in the last 10 league games – an average of 0.5 per game compared to 1.4 for the 10 matches before. Only Manchester United, with a 0.4 average, have a better record over the same period.

FA CARLING PREMIERSHIP

SATURDAY 3/2/01
LIVERPOOL 3 Smicer 20, Fowler 45, 57
WEST HAM 0

SATURDAY 10/2/01
SUNDERLAND 1 Hutchison 51
LIVERPOOL 1 Litmanen 79pen

IN THE LEAGUE **SATURDAY 3/2/01 TO SATURDAY 10/2/01**

LIGHT FANTASTIC

Just time for Robbie and
the team to catch breath

WE SHALL NOT BE MOVED

O ne down, two to go. A top-three finish in the Premiership remains the priority, but it's hard not to get carried away by the storming form that has already landed one cup and propelled Liverpool into the quarter-finals of two more. "The fact the Worthington Cup is in the cabinet should inspire us to win more honours," predicts club captain Jamie Redknapp.

A tricky tie at Tranmere Rovers is next in the FA Cup, sandwiched between two tasty Uefa Cup clashes with Porto. And if the schedule isn't hectic enough already, there's also international duty looming. England coach and confirmed Reds fan Sven Goran Eriksson has half-a-dozen Liverpool players in mind for the squad to face a Finnish team featuring Sami Hyypia and Jari Litmanen at Anfield on Saturday 24 March, closely followed by a second World Cup qualifier against Albania in Tirana. Still, at least the month ends on a quiet note. Supercharged morning kick-off against Manchester United, anyone?

SATURDAY 3/3/01
LEICESTER CITY (A) **PREMIERSHIP**

THURSDAY 8/3/01
PORTO (A) **UEFA CUP QF 1L**

SUNDAY 11/3/01
TRANMERE ROVERS (A) **FA CUP QF**

THURSDAY 15/3/01
PORTO (H) **UEFA CUP QF 2L**

SUNDAY 18/3/01
DERBY COUNTY (H) **PREMIERSHIP**

SATURDAY 31/3/01
MANCHESTER UNITED (H) **PREMIERSHIP**

GOOD NICK

PORTO 0
LIVERPOOL 0

LINE UP

55 OVCHINNIKOV
2 JORGE COSTA
3 NELSON
5 PAREDES
7 SECRETARIO
10 DECO
11 DRULOVIC
13 ANDRADE
18 CHAINHO
32 CAPUCHO
31 PENA

SUBSTITUTES
44 ESPINHA
4 ALOISIO
  Jorge Costa 58
20 SANTOS
25 CANDIDO COSTA
  Drulovic 70
23 MARIC
27 ROMEU
28 CLAYTON

BOOKING
PAREDES

1 WESTERVELD
6 BABBEL
2 HENCHOZ
12 HYYPIA
23 CARRAGHER
3 ZIEGE
16 HAMANN
17 GERRARD
7 SMICER
10 OWEN
9 FOWLER

SUBSTITUTES
19 ARPHEXAD
29 WRIGHT
13 MURPHY
  Ziege 55
21 McALLISTER
20 BARMBY
  Owen 80
8 HESKEY
  Fowler 69
24 DIOMEDE

Nick Barmby evades the challenge of Porto's Deco

On a torrential night in Portugal, Liverpool soaked up the pressure superbly as Gérard Houllier's men enjoyed a classic European away day.

The Reds had to survive a second-half siege from Porto, but with Sami Hyypia and Stephane Henchoz in top form at the back, they never really looked like caving in and thoroughly deserved to take a 0-0 draw back to Anfield for the second leg.

Liverpool appeared the more likely to break the deadlock, with both Robbie Fowler and Michael Owen looking sharp upfront. On 20 minutes, some neat play between Vladimir Smicer and Jamie Carragher enabled Owen to deliver a low left-foot cross towards Fowler, but the ball was scrambled away by Jorge Andrade. Four minutes later, Fowler's deft touch let Owen test Sergei Ovchinnikov with a low drive.

Porto stormed forward after the break, nearly going in front after Capucho wriggled clear and steered in an inviting cross towards Jesus Pena, only for Henchoz to extinguish the danger. Minutes later, the Swiss defender blocked a Deco effort.

It wasn't until the second half that the Reds had their first attempt on goal, from the impressive Steven Gerrard, who fired a half-volley towards the bottom corner, but he was denied with an excellent save by Ovchinnikov.

Pena missed an easy chance to win the game for Porto minutes later, but he snatched at his shot and sent the ball wide, an error he repeated 10 minutes from time when his low right-foot drive fizzed wide of the Liverpool goal.

The manager was quick to downplay over confidence for the return leg, however. "I still don't rate our chances as better than 50-50," Houllier said. "They can still break us. Porto possess sufficient quality to score at our place."

83
The percentage of Jamie Carragher's passes that reached another Red

- **Reds earn draw on a torrential night**
- **Porto come out attacking in second half**
- **Stephane Henchoz rock solid at the back**

THOMMO'S VERDICT

"Porto went into this game with an extremely impressive home record and when you combined that with the atrocious weather, we knew it was going to be a really tough night.

"We started off confidently, both attacking and defending well and could have gone in at half time ahead after Robbie had a great effort cleared off the line.

"They had a good spell after the break and showed they're a tidy footballing side. But we felt more than capable of coping with the pressure they put on us. In the end it was an honourable draw and a night for the defences to be pleased with themselves. I don't like to single out players because all the lads deserve credit, but Stephane Henchoz in particular was superb, making crucial blocks and tackles all night. We looked ahead to the second leg with caution though, aware Porto could sneak one away from home."

LIVERPOOL OFFICIAL MATCHDAY MAGAZINE
MAN OF THE MATCH STEPHANE HENCHOZ

Team line-up (graphic)

Robbie FOWLER
Michael OWEN

Christian ZIEGE
Dietmar HAMANN
Steven GERRARD
Vladimir SMICER

Jamie CARRAGHER
Sami HYYPIA
Stephane HENCHOZ
Markus BABBEL

Sander WESTERVELD

DO THEY MEAN US?

"The stalemate has given Liverpool an excellent platform on which to build. Few at the Merseyside club would have failed to realise that they are potentially only three matches away from their first European final for over 15 years"
Alex Hayes
The Independent

"At the age of 20, Gerrard keeps on growing. And I'm not talking about the odd inch. Against Porto he showed exactly why he's rated one of the great hopes of England's future. This is one boy who can do a big job for Sven Goran Eriksson. In Europe's city of culture for the year 2001, Gerrard was as classy as they come"
David Moore
The Mirror

"Steven Gerrard dazzled Portugal last night. The 20-year-old's assurance in the eye of a storm in the Estadio Das Antas captivated an audience which included England coach Sven Goran Eriksson. Gerrard has been hailed as England captain, let alone the mainstay of midfield"
John Edwards *Daily Mail*

Acrobatics as Stephane Henchoz tangles with Pena

TRANMERE ROVERS 2 *Yates 46 Allison 58*
LIVERPOOL 4 *Murphy 11 Owen 27 Gerrard 52 Fowler 81pen*

LINE UP

1 ACHTERBERG
18 HINDS
15 ALLEN
31 JOBSON
2 YATES
9 PARKINSON
8 HENRY
16 KOUMAS
3 ROBERTS
25 RIDEOUT
11 BARLOW

SUBSTITUTES
13 MURPHY
10 TAYLOR
5 CHALLINOR
   Jobson 60
12 MORGAN
4 ALLISON
   Rideout 57

BOOKED
ALLEN
HENRY
ROBERTS

1 WESTERVELD
29 WRIGHT
6 BABBEL
12 HYYPIA
23 CARRAGHER
20 BARMBY
21 McALLISTER
17 GERRARD
13 MURPHY
9 FOWLER
10 OWEN

SUBSTITUTES
19 ARPHEXAD
27 VIGNAL
25 BISCAN
   Barmby 66
7 SMICER
   Murphy 83
37 LITMANEN
   Owen 87

Steven Gerrard's close-range header restored Liverpool's two-goal advantage

Tranmere may have been languishing at the bottom of Division One, but for Liverpool, this FA Cup fixture was every bit as difficult as their previous ties against Premiership giants Leeds and Manchester City.

Not only were Rovers eager to take the scalp of their bigger neighbours, but the Wirral side had developed a reputation as giant killers, having already seen off Southampton and Everton. Also, Tranmere boss John Aldridge was relishing the chance

29

The number of clearances, blocks and interceptions by Sami Hyypia

to dump his old club out of the FA Cup. "It's not just another game," he said. "This is much bigger than another cup tie."

Gérard Houllier was in no mood for an upset, however, and Liverpool set about their task with discipline from the start. The Reds took the lead on 11 minutes, Michael Owen teeing up a Danny Murphy header that Tranmere keeper John Achterberg will feel he should have saved. Murphy returned the compliment for Owen a quarter of an hour later, angling a pass for the forward to drill home. With the Reds

cruising, and Gary McAllister and Steven Gerrard controlling the midfield, it looked like game over. But a Rovers goal within a minute of the restart brought the game back to life, as Steve Yates headed in Jason Koumas' cross.

Liverpool nerves were settled by Gerrard, who retaliated with a point-blank header to restore the two-goal lead, but a wayward Robbie Fowler back pass gave the home side hope as Wayne Allison latched on to it to score.

However, Gary Mac's surging run settled the match when he was brought down illegally by Yates. Fowler coolly converted the resultant penalty to set up a semi-final clash with Wycombe.

Murphy heads home opener on return
Fowler spot-kick seals semi-final berth
Gerrard and McAllister shine in midfield

Robbie **FOWLER**   Michael **OWEN**

Danny **MURPHY**   Steven **GERRARD**   Gary **McALLISTER**   Nick **BARMBY**

Jamie **CARRAGHER**   Sami **HYYPIA**   Markus **BABBEL**   Stephen **WRIGHT**

Sander **WESTERVELD**

LIVERPOOL OFFICIAL MATCHDAY MAGAZINE
MAN OF THE MATCH **DANNY MURPHY**

THOMMO'S VERDICT

"I really wanted to congratulate the players on this performance, because there were so many factors making this a difficult tie. We conditioned the lads for a real battle, and went into it with the same approach as we would a European or Premiership match. You have to give Tranmere respect. They really bombard you and it is no wonder they have taken so many Premiership scalps.

"On top of that, this was the one scalp they really wanted and they had nothing to lose. We defended magnificently and managed to create and take our own chances. There were moments when it looked like Tranmere might get back into the game, but we fought back with total commitment to run out winners.

"Danny Murphy was absolutely superb coming back from injury, and the back four stayed disciplined all afternoon. It was a fantastic display by the lads."

Danny Murphy silences the Prenton Park crowd after 11 minutes with a header

LIVERPOOL 2 *Murphy 33   Owen 38*
PORTO 0

LINE UP

1 WESTERVELD
6 BABBEL
2 HENCHOZ
12 HYYPIA
23 CARRAGHER
17 GERRARD
16 HAMANN
13 MURPHY
7 SMICER
10 OWEN
9 FOWLER

SUBSTITUTES
19 ARPHEXAD
29 WRIGHT
3 ZIEGE
Murphy 87
21 McALLISTER
24 DIOMEDE
37 LITMANEN
Smicer 73
8 HESKEY
Fowler 73

BOOKED
GERRARD

44 ESPINHA
7 SECRETARIO
33 SILVA
13 ANDRADE
3 NELSON
20 SANTOS
5 PAREDES
15 ALENITCHEV
25 CANDIDO COSTA
31 PENA
29 CRUZ

SUBSTITUTES
55 OVCHINIKOV
4 ALOISIO
21 NUNO
Secretario 46
23 MARIC
Santos 79
10 DECO
Candido Costa 46
11 DRULOVIC
18 CHAINHO
32 CAPUCHO

BOOKED
SILVA, SECRETARIO, CRUZ

Danny Murphy despatches Liverpool's first goal of the night, and 12th of the Uefa campaign

- **Michael Owen runs the Porto defence ragged**
- **A cautious start gives way to commanding lead**
- **Oscar-winning performance from Carlos Secretario**

LIVERPOOL 2 *Murphy 33 Owen 38*
PORTO 0

Michael Owen was on blistering form as he destroyed Porto practically single-handedly to book Liverpool's spot in the semi-finals and keep them on course for a cup treble.

Within minutes of the kick-off Owen was showing the visitors exactly what he can do, tearing through their defence and causing all kinds of trouble that led to a crude challenge from Ricardo Silva, who was first in referee Kim Nielsen's book. Owen was unlucky not to score after a cheeky turn and chip that nearly caught out keeper Pedro Espinha

as it threatened to drop under his crossbar, while the industrious Steven Gerrard hit a thunderous half-volley from 35 yards that Espinha did well to palm over.

A lingering memory of the night, and one defender Carlos Secretario will want to forget, came almost on the half hour when he hauled down Owen just outside the area, but writhed around for four minutes seemingly in an attempt to avoid punishment for the foul. It was to no avail as the Danish referee, tired of his antics, booked him for feigning injury. The boos from the Kop for the rest of

the half told their own story.

Liverpool took the lead soon after. Gerrard played in a deep cross that eluded everyone except Danny Murphy who controlled and finished in immaculate fashion. Owen scored the second five minutes later to secure Liverpool's passage into the last four. Gerrard again was the provider, whipping the ball in from the right for Owen to leap up and nod home.

"There are teams that will now be wary of meeting Liverpool," said Gérard Houllier. "We had a strategy, developed it and grew in confidence after our goals."

Porto's Pedro Espinha is left stranded as Michael Owen's header hits the top corner

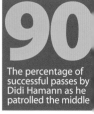

90

The percentage of successful passes by Didi Hamann as he patrolled the middle

"There are teams that will now be wary of meeting Liverpool. We had a strategy, developed it and grew in confidence after scoring our goals"
Gérard Houllier

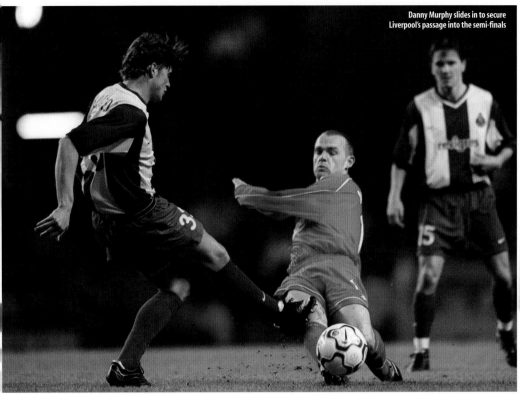
Danny Murphy slides in to secure Liverpool's passage into the semi-finals

LIVERPOOL OFFICIAL MATCHDAY MAGAZINE
MAN OF THE MATCH **DANNY MURPHY**

Robbie **FOWLER** Michael **OWEN**

Vladimir **SMICER** Danny **MURPHY** Dietmar **HAMANN** Steven **GERRARD**

Jamie **CARRAGHER** Sami **HYYPIA** Stephane **HENCHOZ** Markus **BABBEL**

Sander **WESTERVELD**

THOMMO'S VERDICT

"It was another fabulous European night at Anfield, a great atmosphere and a great result. It was a bit nervy at first because we had no away goal, so it was very important to maintain our concentration. We knew we had to attack and be positive, but also be very aware at the back and not do anything silly.

"Porto had generally been scoring away from home all season so we did well to keep them at bay.

"Our goals weren't really top-draw stuff, but we cared far more about the result than how we put the ball in the net. Danny Murphy made an excellent return from injury to have an exceptional game. Michael Owen also played very well and constantly threatened them. He could have got more than one.

"The crowd gave us a real lift once again, got behind us from the off and we were very grateful for that."

UNITED THEY FALL

Danny shoots over, but the Reds
complete the double over United

After the glory of Cardiff,
Liverpool come down to
earth with a bump in a
2-0 reverse at Filbert
Street that Phil Thompson calls
"the kind of game we need to
grind out results in." There's
more frustration the Sunday after
the euphoric Uefa Cup second
leg win over Porto, when in their
first home Premiership game for
six weeks the Reds draw with
Derby County and slip down to
sixth in the table. A week later,
Jari Litmanen is ruled out of
action for six weeks with a
fractured wrist sustained in the
England-Finland game, but his
bad news is tempered by the
return of Patrik Berger in the
terrific 2-0 win over Manchester
United that sends shockwaves
through the League and pushes
Liverpool back up to fourth.
"We all sensed we were going to
win," says goalscorer Steven
Gerrard. "We're definitely
closing the gap on them."

FA CARLING PREMIERSHIP

SATURDAY 3/3/01
LEICESTER CITY 2 Akinbiyi 50, Izzet 90
LIVERPOOL 0

SUNDAY 18/3/01
LIVERPOOL 1 Owen 52
DERBY COUNTY 1 Burton 9

SATURDAY 31/3/01
LIVERPOOL 2 Gerrard 16, Fowler 41
MANCHESTER UNITED 0

Gary Mac steps up to send
José Reina the wrong way

WHO LET THE REDS OUT?

It's starting to get serious, as the unlikely combination of Barcelona and Wycombe Wanderers stand between Liverpool and another two finals.

But Gérard Houllier isn't happy that a Premiership fixture pile-up threatens Liverpool's treble bid. "I don't agree with the fixtures," he says. "I am not going to let my players be treated in the same way people treat horses."

Barça skipper Pep Guardiola is fired up by the prospect of playing at Anfield, meanwhile. "Playing on a mythical stage like Anfield is still like a dream come true," says the midfielder.

And Wycombe boss Lawrie Sanchez is rubbing his hands at the chance to wreck Liverpool's FA Cup chances, just as he did for Wimbledon 13 years ago…

THURSDAY 5/4/01
BARCELONA (A) **UEFA CUP SF 1L**

SUNDAY 8/4/01
WYCOMBE WANDERERS (VILLA PARK)
FA CUP SF

TUESDAY 10/4/01
IPSWICH TOWN (A) **PREMIERSHIP**

FRIDAY 13/4/01
LEEDS UNITED (H) **PREMIERSHIP**

MONDAY 16/4/01
EVERTON (A) **PREMIERSHIP**

THURSDAY 19/4/01
BARCELONA (H) **UEFA CUP SF 2L**

SUNDAY 22/4/01
TOTTENHAM HOTSPUR (H) **PREMIERSHIP**

SATURDAY 28/4/01
COVENTRY CITY (A) **PREMIERSHIP**

TUESDAY 1/5/01
BRADFORD CITY (A) **PREMIERSHIP**

SATURDAY 5/5/01
NEWCASTLE UNITED (H) **PREMIERSHIP**

TUESDAY 8/5/01
CHELSEA (H) **PREMIERSHIP**

BARCELONA 0
LIVERPOOL 0

Barça's Patrick Kluivert gets to grips with Dietmar Hamann

Gérard Houllier showed all his mastery of the tactical side of European football as Liverpool ground out a superb draw in the Nou Camp against one of the world's best attacking forces. The Reds became only the second team all season to stop Barça from scoring at home. Markus Babbel, Sami Hyypia, Stephane Henchoz and Jamie Carragher soaked up all the pressure the Catalan side could throw at them, while Didi Hamann and Steven Gerrard fought for every ball in the middle of the park.

In a tactical change designed to stifle Barcelona's counterattacking play, Emile Heskey was deployed on the left-hand side of a five-man midfield, leaving Michael Owen to battle alone upfront. As a plan, it proved a resounding success with Rivaldo and his colleagues reduced to taking long-range pot shots in frustration.

Only twice in the first-half was the assured Reds defence threatened. A Rivaldo shot was deflected wide by an outstretched Hyypia, and the Brazilian's header down to Luis Enrique resulted in a wayward shot.

Liverpool's spirit and last-ditch tackles kept them in the game in the second period, as Carragher twice blocked Luis Enrique attempts, and Sander Westerveld wasn't tested until Xavi's long-range curler in the dying minutes.

The failure to score resulted in the home crowd whistling their own side in frustration and great satisfaction for the Anfield contingent at full time.

A satisfied Houllier dismissed claims from Barcelona and sections of the media that Liverpool had spoilt the game with negative play. "Perhaps we respected them a little too much," he said. "But I didn't want us to get unbalanced. I'm not going to apologise for stopping them scoring."

69
clearances, blocks and interceptions made by the Reds XI on the night

- **Reds wear white as they stop Rivaldo and co**
- **Defiant defence keeps Euro dream going**
- **Frustrated home fans boo Barça off the pitch**

A rock-solid performance at the back from Stephane Henchoz

DO THEY MEAN US?

"It may not have carried the drama of the EastEnders shooting, but Liverpool's ruthless strangulation of Barcelona was captivating in its own way. Past performances in Catalonia mean this should not be discounted. Alex Ferguson has seen his side throw away a lead here, while Leeds were given a torrid initiation this season"
Ian McGarry *Daily Mail*

BARCELONA 0 LIVERPOOL 0

Liverpool dream kept alive by the thin white line

"Liverpool emerged unscathed from the Nou Camp having frustrated Barcelona with an outstanding defensive display. There has been no greater improvement with a rearguard whose new-found qualities of resilience and composure left groans of the home support lingering into the night"
Paul Joyce *Daily Express*

"No goals, no action, no shots in anger. It was classic Liverpool in their heyday, soaking up the pressure in search of a clean sheet to take to Anfield. You can't ask for better in the Nou Camp"
David Maddock *The Mirror*

LIVERPOOL OFFICIAL MATCHDAY MAGAZINE
MAN OF THE MATCH STEPHANE HENCHOZ

Michael OWEN
Emile HESKEY
Patrik BERGER   Steven GERRARD   Dietmar HAMANN   Danny MURPHY
Jamie CARRAGHER   Sami HYYPIA   Stephane HENCHOZ   Markus BABBEL
Sander WESTERVELD

THOMMO'S VERDICT

"The Nou Camp is an absolutely magnificent setting. Our fans were spread around the ground but still made themselves heard among the Catalans, which helped us a lot.

"Our main aim was to keep a clean sheet. The lads gave a superb, battling display, full of discipline and character. We didn't keep the ball as well as we could have done at times, but the defensive side of our game was excellent, from the keeper through to the forwards.

"Steven and Didi did a great job in front of the defence and Sander only had one real save to make, which is an achievement against a side like Barça. They're always likely to score at home, but we contained them to the degree that the crowd was getting really frustrated.

"That match gave us a real chance in the return leg at Anfield, where we knew we'd have to go out and play more offensively."

WYCOMBE WANDERERS 1 *Ryan 88*
LIVERPOOL 2 *Heskey 78 Fowler 83*

LINE UP

W.W.F.C.

1 TAYLOR
4 COUSINS
3 VINNICOMBE
5 McCARTHY
6 BATES
8 RYAN
18 TOWNSEND
28 SIMPSON
30 BROWN
16 RAMMELL
22 BULMAN

SUBSTITUTES
26 OSBORNE
25 LEE
7 CARROLL
Townsend 81
24 WHITTINGHAM
Brown 81
36 ESSANDOH
Rammell 56

BOOKED
BROWN
COUSINS

1 WESTERVELD
6 BABBEL
23 CARRAGHER
2 HENCHOZ
12 HYYPIA
16 HAMANN
20 BARMBY
21 McALLISTER
3 ZIEGE
9 FOWLER
10 OWEN

SUBSTITUTES
19 ARPHEXAD
17 GERRARD
Barmby 51
15 BERGER
13 MURPHY
Owen 81
8 HESKEY
Ziege 61

Robbie Fowler curls his 83rd minute free-kick into the net

- **Class prevails in soggy semi-final showdown**
- **Heskey breaks deadlock with diving header**
- **Fowler's stunner seals second trip to Cardiff**

WYCOMBE WANDERERS 1 *Ryan 88*
LIVERPOOL 2 *Heskey 78 Fowler 83*

The FA Cup semi-final, much like the sixth-round tie at Tranmere, was a potential banana skin for Liverpool. Fresh from beating Manchester United at Anfield, and keeping a clean sheet at the Nou Camp, the Reds faced a giantkilling Wycombe side intent on bringing Liverpool crashing back down to earth at Villa Park.

To add spice to the occasion, Wycombe boss Lawrie Sanchez taunted Liverpool by claiming his 1988 FA Cup final winning goal for Wimbledon had brought about the beginning of the end of Anfield's golden era. Gérard

Houllier set out to prove a new one was on its way.

It was never easy for Liverpool. Wycombe's back three of Jamie Bates, Jason Cousins and Paul McCarthy defended with the sort of determination the Reds had displayed in Catalunya three days earlier, while Liverpool's rearguard was equally resilient and goalscoring chances were few and far between. Michael Owen spurned one rare opportunity in the 33rd minute, clipping the ball at the advancing Martin Taylor.

The second half saw Wycombe threaten less, as Liverpool's greater stamina increased their

influence, while Steven Gerrard's arrival added steel to the midfield.

The first corner of the match, on 78 minutes, saw Gary McAllister roll the ball to Gerrard, whose powerful dipping cross was met by Emile Heskey to give Liverpool the lead at last.

Robbie Fowler then added a cracking goal from a free-kick to put the result beyond doubt. Wycombe kept going, however, and with two minutes left, striker Keith Ryan lobbed in to give his side's fans something to cheer. But it was too late to change the result, and the Reds marched into their first FA Cup final since 1996.

Emile Heskey celebrates the strike that broke the deadlock at Villa Park

57
The number of passes Sami Hyypia made to one of his team-mates

"Half the country wanted Wycombe Wanderers to win. They rose to
the occasion but we did enough to get through"

Gérard Houllier

Robbie
FOWLER

Michael
OWEN

Christian
ZIEGE

Gary
McALLISTER

Dietmar
HAMANN

Nick
BARMBY

Jamie
CARRAGHER

Sami
HYYPIA

Stephane
HENCHOZ

Markus
BABBEL

Sander
WESTERVELD

LIVERPOOL OFFICIAL MATCHDAY MAGAZINE
MAN OF THE MATCH SAMI HYYPIA

THOMMO'S VERDICT

"We knew it would be a tough nut to crack but we were determined to disprove some of the reports in the press suggesting Liverpool wouldn't compete as hard as Wycombe. We were just as hungry as them, and we stayed disciplined throughout as they threw everything they had at us. They defended with great determination and succeeded in frustrating us for a good while.

"Patience was the key, as we are always stressing to our players, and we eventually wore them down. Emile, Stevie and Danny came on as substitutes and their exceptional pace and power turned the screw. It was a good set piece for the first goal and Robbie Fowler finished the game off with a real beauty of a free-kick.

"It was a fantastic result and to reach our second cup final of the season was beyond what any of us could have expected when we kicked off in August."

DO THEY MEAN US?

"We spent a lot of time defending, but you expect to have to do that against Liverpool. We restricted them to a few chances and it wasn't until near the end that they started to get behind us. If you're going out of a competition then the best way to go is to score a goal and have a side like Liverpool on the back foot for the final few minutes, as we did"
Wycombe manager, Lawrie Sanchez

Heskey ends Wycombe's dream

"Wycombe defended just as Liverpool had done at the Nou Camp, as if far more than a cup final place was at stake. Houllier responded by releasing one of his strikers from the bench. His objective was perfectly clear. End this torture as quickly as possible"
Matt Lawton
The Daily Telegraph

"When Wycombe succumbed in the last 13 minutes, their tongues hanging out with exhaustion, it was because the great class divide told. Liverpool deserve their place against Arsenal in Cardiff, but they will know that the journeymen from Buckinghamshire had bravely submitted their all"
Steve Curry *Daily Mail*

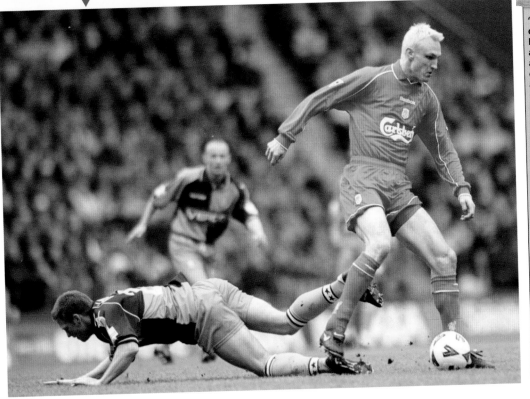

LIVERPOOL 1 *McAllister 44pen*
BARCELONA 0

LINE UP

LIVERPOOL

1 WESTERVELD
6 BABBEL
2 HENCHOZ
12 HYYPIA
23 CARRAGHER
17 GERRARD
16 HAMANN
21 McALLISTER
7 SMICER
8 HESKEY
10 OWEN

SUBSTITUTES
19 ARPHEXAD
27 VIGNAL
29 WRIGHT
3 ZIEGE
13 MURPHY
Gerrard 78
15 BERGER
Owen 62
9 FOWLER
Smicer 80

BOOKED
WESTERVELD

35 REINA
2 REIZIGER
3 DE BOER
24 PUYOL
17 PETIT
21 LUIS ENRIQUE
8 COCU
4 GUARDIOLA
11 OVERMARS
9 KLUIVERT
10 RIVALDO

SUBSTITUTES
1 DUTRUEL
23 ZENDEN
20 SIMAO
Reiziger 59
6 DE LA PEÑA
16 XAVI
18 GABRI
19 DANI
Overmars 74

BOOKED
SIMAO

Patrick Kluivert watches Gary McAllister celebrate the penalty he gave away

Gary McAllister was the ice-cool penalty hero for Liverpool as he helped see off the Catalan giants and guided the Reds into their first European final in 16 years.

On a night of passion at Anfield, the Scot grabbed the headlines for the second time in four days, after his late, late winner at Everton.

It was a measure of how far the team have come under Gérard Houllier that they were able to defeat a side containing the likes of Patrick Kluivert and Rivaldo, arguably the world's best player.

The Brazilian showed what he can do after just seven minutes. Picking up a loose ball from Vladimir Smicer 45 yards out, he took one look up and struck a blistering shot. But Sander Westerveld scrambled back and pushed the ball to safety. Michael Owen, Sami Hyypia and Smicer all went close for Liverpool, while Luis Enrique couldn't connect properly with Marc Overmars' cross and his effort crept wide.

The turning point arrived just before the interval, when Kluivert inexplicably met the ball with his right hand following McAllister's corner. Referee Urs Meier pointed to the spot, and the Scot stepped up to send the ball to José Reina's left.

Liverpool looked assured in the second half, except for one moment when

Emmanuel Petit played Kluivert through, and although it seemed a simple enough ball for Westerveld to clear, he connected with nothing but air. Luckily, his Holland team-mate was unable to retrieve the ball and, to everyone's relief, it trickled out.

The night was summed up when Rivaldo was sent sprawling by the magnificent Hyypia, as the Reds enjoyed victory over a team who'd dismissed our defensive display at the Nou Camp a fortnight earlier.

"They rubbished us after that first game," said a delighted McAllister. "But they're out and we are through."

9
The number of crucial tackles made by defender Stephane Henchoz

- **McAllister's penalty sees off Catalan giants**
- **Defensive heroics from Henchoz and Hyypia**
- **Rivaldo and Kluivert effectively shackled**

Emile HESKEY   Michael OWEN

Vladimir SMICER   Gary McALLISTER   Dietmar HAMANN   Steven GERRARD

Jamie CARRAGHER   Sami HYYPIA   Stephane HENCHOZ   Markus BABBEL

Sander WESTERVELD

LIVERPOOL OFFICIAL MATCHDAY MAGAZINE
MAN OF THE MATCH STEPHANE HENCHOZ

THOMMO'S VERDICT

"Nights like this at Anfield don't come much bigger than this. People always talk about the famous St Etienne game but this rivalled it in terms of passion and commitment. The disrespectful criticism from Barcelona following the first leg doubly fired us up. Every one of our players was outstanding. The first 45 minutes belonged to the forwards and the second half to the defence.

"We caused them all sorts of problems attacking in the first half, and the goal came at just the right time – Gary McAllister took the penalty very well. Barça came out all guns blazing in the second half as we thought they would, and we performed defensive heroics. To limit the likes of Rivaldo and Patrick Kluivert to so few chances is amazing and a testimony to our players.

"It was a magical, wonderful night, and much of the credit has to go to our fans who were also magnificent."

Gérard Houllier congratulates Henchoz on his star performance

RELENTLESS

Eight Premiership games in less than a month – not counting the visit of Barcelona and two cup finals? Piece of cake. Strangely, losing at home to fellow Champions League chasers Leeds proves to be the catalyst. But it's Gary Mac's sensational late winner at Everton that really lights the fuse as the Reds acquire an air of invincibility, winning four on the bounce and drawing with Chelsea to set up a grand finale at Charlton. "Gary's goal has given us control over our destiny," says the boss. "I'm sure some doubters are waiting for us to trip, but that's not going to happen again."

FA CARLING PREMIERSHIP

TUESDAY 10/4/01
IPSWICH TOWN 1 Armstrong 77
LIVERPOOL 1 Heskey 46

FRIDAY 13/4/01
LIVERPOOL 1 Gerrard 54
LEEDS UNITED 2 Ferdinand 4, Bowyer 33

MONDAY 16/5/01
EVERTON 2 Ferguson 42, Unsworth 83pen
LIVERPOOL 3 Heskey 4, Babbel 56, McAllister 90

SATURDAY 31/1/01
LIVERPOOL 3 Heskey 6, McAllister 72pen, Fowler 88
TOTTENHAM HOTSPUR 1 Korsten 22

SATURDAY 28/4/01
COVENTRY CITY 0
LIVERPOOL 2 Hyypia 84, McAllister 86

TUESDAY 1/5/01
BRADFORD CITY 0
LIVERPOOL 2 Owen 47, McAllister 67

SATURDAY 5/5/01
LIVERPOOL 3 Owen 25 72 81
NEWCASTLE UNITED 0

TUESDAY 8/5/01
LIVERPOOL 2 Owen 8 60
CHELSEA 2 Hasselbaink 13 67

FINAL FRONTIER

Owen strikes like a cobra. Arsenal will be history in less than 10 minutes

What a way to end the season. After 60 games, Liverpool stand on the threshold of history, ready to surpass all that they've achieved in the preceding 10 years. But whatever happens against Arsenal, Alavés and Charlton, it's already been a phenomenal campaign. The Reds are about to become the first team ever to complete every fixture possible in a season. They've scored 116 goals and failed to find the net in only eight games. They can now become the first team to win the FA Cup outside England, while victory in Dortmund will make them the first British club to win the Uefa Cup three times and Gérard Houllier the first Frenchman to win a European trophy with a foreign side. Amid all the excitement, the boss pays a heartfelt tribute to the fans: "I know it's not cheap following the team to so many different games, but we owe you for your backing. It's together we'll take this club forward to further success."

SATURDAY 12/5/01
ARSENAL (MILLENNIUM STADIUM)
FA CUP FINAL

WEDNESDAY 16/5/01
ALAVÉS (WESTFALENSTADION)
UEFA CUP FINAL

SATURDAY 19/5/01
CHARLTON ATHLETIC (A) **PREMIERSHIP**

ARSENAL 1 *Ljungberg 72*
LIVERPOOL 2 *Owen 82 88*

LINE UP

1 SEAMAN
2 DIXON
5 KEOWN
6 ADAMS
29 COLE
7 PIRES
4 VIEIRA
18 GRIMANDI
8 LJUNGBERG
11 WILTORD
14 HENRY

SUBSTITUTES
13 MANNINGER
12 LAUREN
15 PARLOUR
Wiltord 75
10 BERGKAMP
Dixon 89
25 KANU
Ljungberg 84

BOOKED
LJUNGBERG

1 WESTERVELD
6 BABBEL
2 HENCHOZ
12 HYYPIA
23 CARRAGHER
13 MURPHY
16 HAMANN
17 GERRARD
7 SMICER
8 HESKEY
10 OWEN

SUBSTITUTES
19 ARPHEXAD
27 VIGNAL
21 McALLISTER
Hamann 60
15 BERGER
Murphy 76
9 FOWLER
Smicer 76

BOOKED
HAMANN

Ee-ay-addio, we've won the cup…

- **Owen at the double in dramatic Cardiff finale**
- **Liverpool fight back after Ljungberg strike**
- **Champagne on ice as Reds win sixth FA Cup**

ARSENAL 1 *Ljungberg 72*
LIVERPOOL 2 *Owen 82 88*

Michael Owen was the hero of the most exciting FA Cup final in years, dramatically grabbing two late goals to snatch the trophy from Arsenal.

With Liverpool trailing 1-0 and seemingly dead and buried at the Millennium Stadium, an amazing six-minute spell of play saw Owen cancel out Freddy Ljungberg's strike and, with just two minutes left and extra time looming, drill home a left-footed shot to take the FA Cup back to Anfield.

Glorious sunshine in Cardiff for the first Cup final to be played outside England meant a carnival atmosphere and energy-sapping conditions for the two teams.

Arsenal started the stronger, with Patrick Vieira orchestrating matters in midfield. The game's most controversial moment came on 17 minutes, when Stephane Henchoz's handball from Thierry Henry's goal-bound shot went unseen by the officials.

The game came to life on the hour, when Henry's close control and ball juggling beat Westerveld but he was denied by a goalline clearance from Sami Hyypia.

By now Liverpool were living dangerously and it was little surprise when, following another scramble off the line by Hyypia, Robert Pires freed Ljungberg who fired home emphatically.

The goal spurred Liverpool on and 10 minutes later Arsenal failed to deal with substitute Gary McAllister's free-kick from the left and Owen half volleyed in the rebound. The Reds were suddenly in control, Owen latching on to a long pass from Patrik Berger, also a sub, muscled past Lee Dixon and threaded a low left-foot drive inside David Seaman's far post.

"I will go to bed every night dreaming about those goals," said Owen afterwards. "It was better than scoring in the World Cup."

Michael Owen leaves David Seaman clutching air and the FA Cup is Liverpool's

90

The percentage of successful passes from Sami Hyypia, a real captain's display

'The Reds borrowed Arsenal's old 'lucky' label. This is no criticism of Liverpool. Houllier is building a side capable of a title challenge"

Henry Winter *The Daily Telegraph*

OPTA'S PLAYER BY PLAYER FA CUP FINAL STATS

Opta @ PLANETFOOTBALL.com

	Gary McALLISTER	Emile HESKEY	Sander WESTERVELD	Stephane HENCHOZ	Vladimir SMICER	Robbie FOWLER	Michael OWEN	Sami HYYPIA	Patrik BERGER	Dietmar HAMANN	Jamie CARRAGHER	Danny MURPHY	Steven GERRARD	Markus BABBEL	TOTAL
TIME ON PITCH	29	90	90	90	78	12	90	90	13	61	90	77	90	90	990
SHOTS															
GOAL SCORED							2								2
SHOT ON TARGET		1			1										2
SHOT OFF TARGET												1	2		3
BLOCKED SHOT		2					1		1	2					6
HIT THE WOODWORK															0
OWN GOAL															0
PASSES															
PASS TO OWN PLAYER	10	12	9	27	14	1	8	38	3	32	36	24	38	34	286
PASS TO OPPOSITION	6	8	6	8	9	3	2	3	1	2		10	8	9	13	88
PASS TO SCORING ZONE (OWN PLAYER)	1											2			3
PASS TO SCORING ZONE (OPPOSITION)	4			2	1	2	1					2	1		13
GOAL ASSIST										1				1	2
PASS COMPLETION	52%	60%	60%	77%	56%	20%	67%	90%	80%	94%	78%	72%	79%	73%	74%
DRIBBLES and RUNS															
POSSESSION RETAINED	2	1			5		3			1	2		2		16
POSSESSION LOST	3			3	3	4			1		2	3	2		21
CONTROLLED FIRST TOUCH														1	1
DRIBBLE SUCCESS	100%	25%	0%	0%	63%	0%	43%	0%	0%	50%	100%	0%	40%	0%	43%
FOULS and FREE-KICKS															
FREE-KICK – FOUL		3		1			2	1		5	1		2	3	18
FREE-KICK – HANDBALL															0
PENALTY CONCEDED															2
FREE-KICK – OFFSIDE		1			1										1
YELLOW CARDS										1					0
RED CARDS															
TACKLES															
TACKLE ATTEMPTED	2	2	0	5	3	0	0	0	1	3	4	6	5	6	37
TACKLE WON	2	2		4	2					1	3	4	5	4	27
TACKLE LOST			1	1					1	2	1	2		2	10
TACKLE SUCCESS RATE	100%	100%	0%	80%	67%	0%	0%	0%	0%	33%	75%	67%	100%	67%	73%
TOTAL TIMES TACKLED		3			3	3	6		2			4	4	2	27
TACKLED, RETAINED POSSESSION							1					2	1		4
TACKLED, LOST POSSESSION		3			3	3	5		2			2	3	2	23
POSSESSION RETENTION RATE	0%	0%	0%	0%	0%	0%	17%	0%	0%	0%	0%	50%	25%	0%	15%
CLEARANCES, BLOCKS, INTERCEPTIONS															
HEADED CLEARANCES		1		5				4		2	3			3	18
OTHER CLEARANCES			1	3				2		2	2		2	1	13
INTERCEPTIONS							1			2		2	1		6
CLEARANCES OFF THE GOAL LINE								2							2
BLOCKED SHOTS										1				1	2
BLOCKED CROSS												2			2
TOTAL TOUCHES	25	30	44	48	36	9	23	53	7	45	59	47	63	62	551

SANDER'S STATS

GOALS CONCEDED	
SHOTS FROM INSIDE BOX	1
SHOTS FROM OUTSIDE BOX	
SHOTS FROM SET PIECE	
SHOTS FROM PENALTY	
ERROR LEADING TO GOAL	
CLEAN SHEET	
SAVES	
SHOTS FROM INSIDE BOX	1
SHOTS FROM OUTSIDE BOX	1
SHOTS FROM SET PIECE	
SHOTS FROM PENALTY	
SMOTHERING THE BALL	
SAVES TO SHOTS RATIO	67%
THROWS	
TOTAL	6
TO OWN PLAYER	6
TO OPPOSITION PLAYER	
THROW COMPLETION RATE	100%
KICKING FROM HANDS and GOAL KICKS	
TOTAL	16
TO OWN PLAYER	4
TO OPPOSITION PLAYER	12
KICKING COMPLETION RATE	25%
KICKING IN OPEN PLAY	
TOTAL	15
TO OWN PLAYER	9
TO OPPOSITION PLATER	6
OPEN PLAY COMPLETION RATE	60%
CATCHING and PUNCHING	
CATCHES	2
PUNCHES	2
BALLS DROPPED	
CROSSES NOT CLAIMED	
CATCH SUCCESS RATE	100%

"UNBELIEVABLE STUFF" John Motson and Mark Lawrenson, BBC

JM This is Berger. Fowler looks sprightly and wants the ball early – but so does Owen! Michael Owen for Liverpool…

Yes! Oh, he's done it! Unbelievable stuff! And Michael Owen might have won the FA Cup for Liverpool!

ML What a piece of opportunism. He hit the ball so early past Seaman. The pace to get past Dixon. Adams turned

him away down the left. He happily went in that direction, though. He knew exactly what he was doing…

ARSENAL 1 *Ljungberg 72*
LIVERPOOL 2 *Owen 82 88*

STRIKE ONE

There were just eight minutes left on referee Steve Dunn's stopwatch when Ray Parlour fouled Jamie Carragher on the left flank.

Substitute Gary McAllister, so lethal from set pieces during Liverpool's treble run-in, curled a free-kick into the box, which skidded off Martin Keown's head, allowing Markus Babbel to leap above Tony Adams at the far post and head the ball back into Michael Owen's path. The striker unleashed a lethal close-range shot across David Seaman's body and into the far corner of the net, to cancel out Freddy Ljungberg's opener.

"I was pleased with the goal," said Owen after the match. "It reminded me of the one against Romania in the World Cup."

"As soon as Michael scored I said we would win it," added manager Gérard Houllier. "He has been like that for a few months now. How can you describe him. Unbelievable."

"If there had been any doubt about Owen's special place in the ame or the strength of his character, it was surely resolved here"

ames Lawton *The Independent*

Sami Hyypia proved Liverpool's saviour

DO THEY MEAN US?

"We should have had a penalty and we're disappointed because the game should have been over before the end. We didn't take our chances. We played well and were the dominant team but we've been punished for not killing Liverpool off"
Arsène Wenger

Owen the goal prince of Wales

"The persistence Liverpool showed brought to mind Arsenal's will to win the championship in 1989. They even borrowed Arsenal's old 'lucky' label. This is no criticism of Liverpool. Gérard Houllier is building a team capable of challenging in the championship marathon"
Henry Winter
The Daily Telegraph

"At the end Henry had been dwarfed by Michael Owen. Great players do not mark out their terrain merely with a series of grace notes. As Owen reminded us so thunderously in winning, almost single-handedly, the FA Cup, effect, not style, is everything. If there had been any doubt about Owen's special place in the game or the strength of his character, it was surely resolved here"
James Lawton
The Independent

VERPOOL OFFICIAL MATCHDAY MAGAZINE
AN OF THE MATCH **SAMI HYYPIA**

Emile **HESKEY**
Michael **OWEN**

Vladimir **SMICER**
Dietmar **HAMANN**
Steven **GERRARD**
Danny **MURPHY**

Jamie **CARRAGHER**
Sami **HYYPIA**
Stephane **HENCHOZ**
Markus **BABBEL**

Sander **WESTERVELD**

THOMMO'S VERDICT

"It was a fantastic day, a tremendous game and contrary to all the talk in the press about Arsenal dominating the match, I felt there was little between the two sides.

"They had some control in spells, but apart from a clean chance for Thierry Henry, they didn't create that much. Sami Hyypia made some vital clearances off the line but then that's his job, being in the right position at the right time. It's not luck, it's outstanding defending.

"Arsenal took the lead but I always felt there was a chance we'd get back into it if we got one-on-one with their defence. And we did, showing plenty of character and togetherness to haul ourselves back in very hot conditions.

"The subs were crucial again in turning the game. We looked more lively and Michael was clinical with his chances. It was a magical day and the celebrations afterwards were amazing."

LIVERPOOL 5 *Babbel 3 Gerrard 15 McAllister 40pen Fowler 72 Geli 116og after extra time*
ALAVÉS 4 *Ivan 26 Moreno 47 50 Cruyff 88*

LINE UP

1 WESTERVELD
6 BABBEL
2 HENCHOZ
12 HYYPIA
23 CARRAGHER
17 GERRARD
13 MURPHY
16 HAMANN
21 McALLISTER
10 OWEN
8 HESKEY

SUBSTITUTES
19 ARPHEXAD
29 WRIGHT
27 VIGNAL
20 BARMBY
7 SMICER
Henchoz 56
15 BERGER
Owen 73
9 FOWLER
Heskey 64

BOOKED
BABBEL

1 HERRERA
7 GELI
2 CONTRA
4 EGGEN
5 KARMONA
6 TELLEZ
16 DESIO
18 ASTUDILLO
15 TOMIC
9 JAVI MORENO
14 CRUYFF

SUBSTITUTES
25 KIKE
19 IVAN ALONSO
Eggen 23
3 IBON BEGONA
17 RAUL GANAN
11 MAGNO
Astudillo 45
20 AZKOITIA
10 PABLO
Javi Moreno 64

BOOKED
ASTUDILLO,
HERRERA,
KARMONA, MAGNO,
TELLEZ

SENT OFF
KARMONA, MAGNO

And the Uefa Cup makes it three...

- **Nine-goal thriller hailed as best-ever final**
- **Brave Alavés finally floored by own-goal**
- **Reds register seventh European trophy**

LIVERPOOL 5 *Babbel 3   Gerrard 15   McAllister 40pen   Fowler 72   Geli 116og after extra time*
ALAVÉS 4 *Ivan 26   Moreno 47 50   Cruyff 88*

In what will surely go down as one of the most exciting finals ever, against brave Alavés, Liverpool completed an unprecedented treble. In a game that swung one way then the other, the Reds secured a 5-4 victory thanks to an extra-time own goal by Delfi Geli. It was Liverpool's seventh European trophy, a total surpassed only by Barcelona and Real Madrid.

Markus Babbel scored with a header after three minutes. Steven Gerrard then latched on to Michael Owen's ball to drive home a second. Game over?

Not quite. Cosmin Contra beat Sander Westerveld with a header, but Liverpool soon restored their advantage. Owen won a penalty and Gary McAllister coolly converted the spot kick.

Straight after the break Javier Moreno made it 3-2 and rapidly added a second with a low free-kick. Robbie Fowler took to the field and on 72 minutes scored the best goal of the game, getting past his marker on the edge of the box to pick his spot. But Alavés fought back again, Jordi Cruyff meeting Contra's header to score.

A frenetic period of extra time saw Magno and Antonio Karmona dismissed for the Spanish side. McAllister stepped up to take a free-kick with three minutes remaining, and Geli headed into his own net.

A magnificent ovation was given to the distraught Alavés players as they collected their medals, and Liverpool's team spirit was demonstrated when joint captains Sami Hyypia and Fowler lifted the trophy together.

"That was an epic," said a delighted Houllier. "We were playing tonight for history, for Liverpool's first European trophy in 17 years. The team played for immortality. Every player will be remembered for a long time."

What a start! German homeboy Markus Babbel heads home Liverpool's first

12

The number of shots on target (8) and off target (4) by the mighty Reds

"They played for immortality. No team will achieve what the Liverpool of old did, but my players wrote their own history out there tonight"

Gérard Houllier

OPTA'S PLAYER BY PLAYER UEFA CUP FINAL STATS

Opta @ PLANETFOOTBALL.com

	Gary McALLISTER	Emile HESKEY	Sander WESTERVELD	Stephane HENCHOZ	Vladimir SMICER	Robbie FOWLER	Michael OWEN	Sami HYYPIA	Patrik BERGER	Dietmar HAMANN	Jamie CARRAGHER	Danny MURPHY	Steven GERRARD	Markus BABBEL	TOTAL
TIME ON PITCH	117	65	117	56	61	52	79	117	38	117	117	117	117	117	1287
SHOTS															
GOAL SCORED	1						1						1	1	4
SHOT ON TARGET												1	2		3
SHOT OFF TARGET		2					1		1	2					6
BLOCKED SHOT															0
HIT THE WOODWORK															0
OWN GOAL															0
PASSES															
PASS TO OWN PLAYER	45	9	9	7	20	12	11	34	13	59	38	40	33	30	360
PASS TO OPPOSITION	8	15	10	3	6	12	3	15	6	11	13	11	11	9	133
PASS TO SCORING ZONE (OWN PLAYER)	1									1					4
PASS TO SCORING ZONE (OPPOSITION)	10	2			1	1						2	4		20
GOAL ASSIST	2														2
PASS COMPLETION	73%	35%	47%	70%	74%	48%	80%	69%	68%	85%	75%	75%	69%	78%	71%
DRIBBLES and RUNS															
POSSESSION RETAINED		2	1			1	2	2	1	3	3	1	2	2	20
POSSESSION LOST	3	2			2	1	2	1	2	1	1	6	1		22
CONTROLLED FIRST TOUCH	2														2
DRIBBLE SUCCESS	40%	33%	0%	0%	50%	67%	33%	50%	60%	75%	25%	67%		0%	48%
FOULS and FREE-KICKS															
FREE-KICK – FOUL															0
FREE-KICK – HANDBALL															3
PENALTY CONCEDED			1												
FREE-KICK – OFFSIDE							1							1	2
YELLOW CARDS	1														1
RED CARDS															0
TACKLES															
TACKLES ATTEMPTED	4	1	0	2	3	0	0	4	2	4	3	5	5	5	38
TACKLE WON	3	1		1	2			3	2	3	2	2	3	3	25
TACKLE LOST	1			1	1			1		1	1	3	2	2	13
TACKLE SUCCESS RATE	75%	100%	0%	50%	67%	0%	0%	75%	100%	75%	67%	40%	60%	60%	66%
TOTAL TIMES TACKLED	6	3			4		2	1	2	2	1	9	1		31
TACKLED, RETAINED POSSESSION	2				1		1			1		2			7
TACKLED, LOST POSSESSION	4	3			3		1	1	2	1	1	7	1		24
POSSESSION RETENTION RATE %	33%	0%	0%	0%	25%	0%	50%	0%	0%	50%	0%	22%	0%	0%	23%
CLEARANCES, BLOCKS, INTERCEPTIONS															
HEADED CLEARANCES				4				9	1		3			8	26
OTHER CLEARANCES			3	1				3			4	1	2	4	18
INTERCEPTIONS							1		1	5	1				8
CLEARANCES OFF THE GOAL LINE															
BLOCKED SHOTS					2					1				3	
BLOCKED CROSS												1			1
TOTAL TOUCHES	81	32	42	17	34	30	19	70	29	86	65	69	61	59	694

SANDER'S STATS

GOALS CONCEDED	
SHOTS FROM INSIDE BOX	3
SHOTS FROM OUTSIDE BOX	
SHOTS FROM SET PIECE	1
SHOTS FROM PENALTY	
ERROR LEADING TO GOAL	
CLEAN SHEET	
SAVES	
SHOTS FROM INSIDE BOX	2
SHOTS FROM OUTSIDE BOX	2
SHOTS FROM SET PIECE	1
SHOTS FROM PENALTY	
SMOTHERING THE BALL	
SAVES TO SHOTS RATIO	56%
THROWS	
TOTAL	2
TO OWN PLAYER	2
TO OPPOSITION PLAYER	
THROW COMPLETION RATE	100%
KICKING FROM HANDS and GOAL KICKS	
TOTAL	10
TO OWN PLAYER	5
TO OPPOSITION PLAYER	5
KICKING COMPLETION RATE	50%
KICKING IN OPEN PLAY	
TOTAL	19
TO OWN PLAYER	9
TO OPPOSITION PLATER	10
OPEN PLAY COMPLETION RATE	47%
CATCHING and PUNCHING	
CATCHES	1
PUNCHES	1
BALLS DROPPED	
CROSSES NOT CLAIMED	
CATCH SUCCESS RATE	100%

"DELIGHT FOR LIVERPOOL!" Barry Davies and Trevor Brooking, BBC

BD And Karmone will go, they're down to nine men, but there are only four minutes and a little more

left. It's had absolutely everything!
TB Can Liverpool conjure something up? They've got four minutes to do it.

BD Five Liverpool players to attack the ball… Oh, it's an own goal! It's a golden goal! McAllister's free-kick,

smile from Gérard Houllier! The golden goal is a delight for Liverpool!
TB Absolutely staggering!

LIVERPOOL 5 *Babbel 3   Gerrard 15   McAllister 40pen   Fowler 72   Geli 116og after extra time*
ALAVÉS 4 *Ivan 26   Moreno 47 50   Cruyff 88*

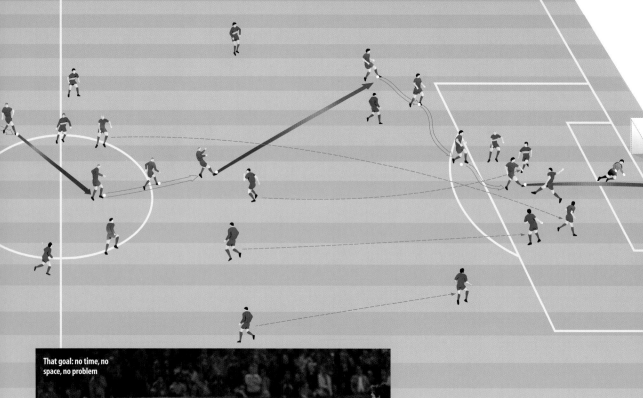

That goal: no time, no space, no problem

ROBBIE FOWLER GOAL 4 ALAVÉS UEFA CUP FINAL

BBC commentator Barry Davies called it *Roy Of The Rovers* stuff, and certainly if anyone deserved a comic-book entrance in Dortmund it was Robbie Fowler. The Kop idol had bided his time the previous Saturday before coming on against Arsenal in Cardiff to make a huge difference. Many Liverpool fans expected him to start against Alavés, but he remained on the bench until the 64th minute when he replaced Emile Heskey with the score locked at 3-3. Eight minutes later, an

Alavés attack broke down and Gary McAllister surged into their half and played a superb ball to Fowler on the end of the box. Surrounded by blue and yellow shirts, Robbie declined to cross and instead cut inside three defenders and danced along the edge of the box before picking his spot with his right foot. "This isn't supposed to happen in European finals!" cried a gleeful Mr Davies. True enough, but then not every European final features a goalscoring genius like Robbie Fowler.

"UNFORGETTABLE"

Robbie Fowler described the Uefa Cup final win that completed Liverpool's treble as, "Nothing short of fantastic. To be honest, I thought I'd got the winning goal when I made the score 4-3 because there wasn't that much time left. At first I didn't know my shot was going in. It was only when I looked at the net and saw the ball there I realised I'd scored. I don't think anyone would have said at the start of the season that Liverpool would clean up in the cups. We're all very pleased and proud of what we've done."

Fellow goalscorer Gary McAllister added, "I'm numb and I can't believe it. This is exactly why I joined. What we achieved here will probably not sink in until after the summer holidays. It's an unforgettable experience."

On a night that eclipsed the following week's dull Champions League final in Milan, the greatest tribute came from Alavés coach José Manuel Esnal, who declared, "We have all shown here that it's footballers who make football great."

'Our attacking play was superb. They were all heroes, but Gary McAllister deserves a special mention. He was just fantastic "

Phil Thompson

Houllier's diamond makes it 3-1 on the night

LIVERPOOL OFFICIAL MATCHDAY MAGAZINE
MAN OF THE MATCH GARY McALLISTER

Emile **HESKEY** Michael **OWEN**

Danny **MURPHY** Dietmar **HAMANN** Gary **McALLISTER** Steven **GERRARD**

Jamie **CARRAGHER** Sami **HYYPIA** Stephane **HENCHOZ** Markus **BABBEL**

Sander **WESTERVELD**

THOMMO'S VERDICT

"There was some annoying talk before the game, about 'little Alavés' who we should be thrashing, and people saying it was going to be the most negative final in history. In the end it turned out to be one of the greatest ever. It was just unbelievable and I was proud to be involved. Once again we made our fans sweat on the result! It's a little disappointing to concede four goals, especially the last one forcing extra time, but in the end our fitness told and our attacking play was superb. They were all heroes, but Gary McAllister deserves a special mention, he was fantastic. The joyful scenes afterwards were incredible, some of the most wonderful seen since 1977 when we won the European Cup for the first time. The fans were magnificent and the way they applauded Alavés, too, show how special they are. A great, great night for the club."

DO THEY MEAN US?

"The game, the fans' behaviour, the atmosphere and the ovation that both teams' supporters gave the Alavés players as they collected their consolation prizes was enough to give you goosebumps. It was truly a match to remember"
Marca Spanish sports newspaper

"Gérard Houllier will take his place alongside Liverpool greats like Bob Paisley, Bill Shankly and Kenny Dalglish after tasting success in the most remarkable European final. It was not sensational football, but it was a sensational football match. Everyone should be absolved of blame for some Sunday league mistakes and just praised for their part in an all-time classic"
Mark Lawrenson

"Liverpool capped their season with a victory from the very soul of football itself, in a match which gave no quarter to those who believed tired legs would undermine the club's march into history. No team has ever won three cups in a season"
Martin Samuel

Is it a bird? Is it a plane? No, it's
Robbie's sensational opener

For five nerve-wracking minutes on the final weekend of the Premiership season, it's Leeds United and not Liverpool heading for the Champions League. At 3.27pm Alan Smith scores against Leicester as the leg-weary Reds struggle to hold Charlton at bay at The Valley. Suddenly, the scheduled open-top bus tour of Liverpool seems something of an anti-climax. Not for long. Following the script to the letter, Gérard Houllier's giants call upon their reserves of character and determination to turn the game on its head in the second half. Once Robbie Fowler breaks the deadlock with a hooked half volley, the Reds run rampant with Danny Murphy, Fowler again and Michael Owen all scoring to end the season in spectacular style. Leeds win 3-1, but it's academic. Liverpool are back where they belong next year – competing with Europe's finest for the first time in 16 years. "It's not been a victory for 11 or 14 players," declares the boss. "It's for the entire squad. When you have the skill and the will, you'll achieve. It's all about mental strength." Roll on next season. The good times are back!

FA CARLING PREMIERSHIP

SATURDAY 19/5/01
CHARLTON ATHLETIC 0
LIVERPOOL 4 Fowler 55, 71, Murphy 61, Owen 80

GLOSS FINISH

BACK HOME

Half a million lining the streets of Liverpool? The team parading in an open-top bus? It's the good times again

Gérard Houllier's all-conquering heroes were welcomed home by a red army of half a million supporters, at the end of a truly unbelievable season.

The triumphant open-topped bus tour of the city was reminiscent of those glorious parades of the 1970s and 1980s, scenes many supporters lining the streets on Sunday 20 May would have been too young to remember. But,

after a long wait, they were able to pay tribute to a new generation of Anfield legends who showed off the FA, Uefa and Worthington Cups. Like the champagne, the celebrations had been put on ice, as the Reds still had to face a crucial final day Premiership trip to Charlton. But with a victory and a Champions League spot in the bag, the party could begin.

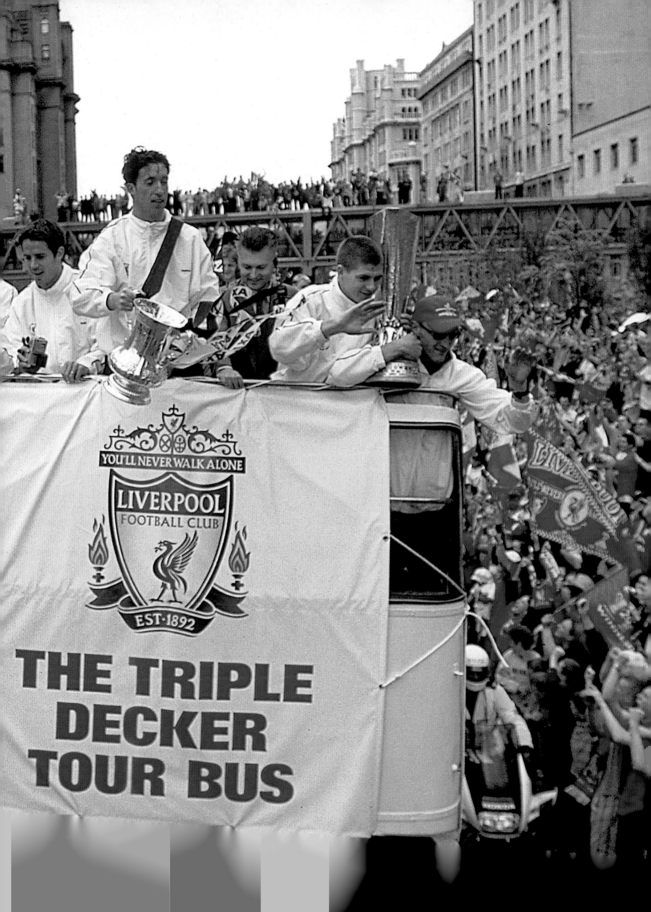

As the players and manager took turns to show off the three trophies, Robbie Fowler said, "I always dreamt of this, going around the city on a bus, waving at the crowds.

"But before this season I'd only won the League Cup and we didn't bother much with that. This is what it's all about. To see so many people standing waving at us, with so much delight on their faces, is fantastic. And this is the start. Believe me, this is the start. There'll be plenty more processions."

The homecoming parade began its two-hour 17-mile circular route near to the team's Melwood training ground, moving on to the city centre and Pier Head, Toxteth, Aigburth, Allerton and Childwall with fans, from toddlers to pensioners, amassed along the way.

Some climbed trees and bus shelters or balanced on chimneys to get a better view while cars followed the cavalcade and others ran and cycled alongside the bus that had two banners hanging from it. One at the front proclaimed it a 'triple decker tour bus' and the one at the back said simply, 'Tell yer Ma – we did it'.

"I've never seen anything like it," said club captain Jamie Redknapp, while first-team coach Sammy Lee, himself a veteran of homecoming tours added, "This is for them. These people are what it's all about."

The last word belonged to Gérard Houllier. "I am happy that the fans are happy," he said. "The achievements of the players have been tremendous. We should not only say well done to the team, but the team behind the team."

SAID AND DONE

THE MIGHTY REDS. IN THEIR OWN WORDS. PLUS ALL THE STATS FROM SEASON 2000/0

JARI LITMANEN

"It's well known I supported Liverpool as a boy in Finland. I had chances to come here before, so when a third one came along, I was determined to sign. It was the right time. I wouldn't want to compare myself to any other player and I wouldn't want to talk about one player in isolation. It's a matter of how well we perform as a team. I mean the entire team – the management, the coaching staff, the back-up, everybody. We've got a very good team here and we will get stronger once we play together a lot. Big European nights, a passionate crowd, the best opposition – this is Liverpool for me."

GARY McALLISTER

"I could hardly believe what was happening in the final week. It was an unbelievable end to the season. But at this club I've learnt that the manager doesn't allow anybody to get above themselves or start drifting too far forward or thinking about their holidays. After the FA Cup final we were training in the morning and talking about Alavés on the Monday.

"The belief in the side stems from getting great results in Barcelona, Rome, Porto and Athens. The young players gained massive experience from results like that and knowing you can go right to the final whistle. We certainly don't think about getting beat.

"Of course, I'd love to have 10 years ahead of me in here because I'm certain Liverpool are going to be a major force again, but for as long as I'm playing, I'll give my all to help this club get back to the top of English football."

MICHAEL OWEN

"People made a lot of me not playing in the Worthington Cup final but the FA Cup final more than made up for it and my winning goal was a nice way to prove those people wrong who'd said I didn't have a left foot. I haven't counted, but I scored a lot with my left foot and my head during the season and it shows I've improved.

"I don't think anyone can doubt the likes of myself, Robbie Fowler or Jamie Carragher when we say we really believe the club is going places. Times have never been as exciting at Liverpool and obviously we want to be part of that because we've been trying to do it for some years. A few of us have been here since we were kids and it'd be brilliant if we could win the League together. If we do well over the coming years, no one will be happier than the local lads who've given 10 to 15 years of their lives to the club."

PATRIK BERGER

"I was always confident I'd come back and it was brilliant to be able to do so in time to play my part in one of the best seasons in the club's history. We didn't win the title but we can definitely build the foundations on which to make a strong challenge next year.

"The Champions League means everything to everyone at Anfield. We've had a taste of playing against the best sides in Europe in the Uefa Cup, and we want it on a regular basis. We've got the players to do it and we can play in a number of ways because tactically we've come on so much in a short space of time. We can play defensively, on the counter-attack, we can take the game to the opposition, we've got pace and lastly, of course, upfront we've got strikers that most clubs in Europe would love to have. I think we'll do well, there's no reason to think otherwise."

DANNY MURPHY

"From a personal point of view, I'll never forget my goal at Old Trafford but you have to move on. It was a special moment for me, but it's in the past now and we have to look to the future – you can't live on one memory for ever. I'm as happy in my career as I've ever been and I need to make sure that doesn't slip and I keep improving.

"The manager said he wanted goals from the midfield and I don't think we let him down. I'm more confident about my game now and not afraid to shoot from distance if the chance arises. I don't have the natural ability to go past people but I can bring people into the game when I've got possession. It's good for me and for my education to play in different positions. People know I felt I'd have to leave Liverpool, but now I've proved what I can do, I just want to improve as much as I can."

STEPHANE HENCHOZ

"The games came thick and fast which is an indication of success but it's also something we got used to. Despite all the big cup ties, the League remained our priority and it was so important we continued to pick points up.

"Sometimes when a team wins after an ordinary display, managers say the result was more important than the performance. But my point is when is it not? Saying that, it's impossible to play badly regularly and win frequently which is why it's important a team's style has a good base. I think we had that base. We have a big, strong squad and I think we felt the benefit of the squad system. We can still improve, too, because we're a young team and we'll get better. Plus, we want to continue rewarding the fans whose support has been magnificent."

SAMI HYYPIA

"Finishing in the top three meant everything and I'm not surprised we did so well in Europe, either. We have a good squad and we're confident in our ability. Some people might not have fancied us to come through against the likes of Barcelona and Roma but after all the work on the training field leading up to those ties, we always knew we'd give both sides a game. And to go on to lift the trophy was a terrific achievement.

"There was talk about the number of games we played but I honestly loved it. Any player will tell you he prefers playing to training and if we have lots of games it means we're doing well and that means the fans are happy. I can't speak highly enough of the fans. Anfield must be an intimidating place to come. Some of the games were unbelievable simply because of the atmosphere. As players you want to perform in the best arenas and Anfield is up there with the very best."

DIETMAR HAMANN

"Early in the season I had a spell on the bench but it's something you have to accept. It's good to have a rhythm and try to improve from week to week, but the manager made it clear he would rest players when necessary and it worked. We have a very big squad at Liverpool and all the players need games. I was very happy with my own form during the run-in and felt confident going into the last week of the season.

"The FA Cup final was the pinnacle of the domestic season and we desperately wanted to win it for the club, the fans and ourselves. But we also desperately wanted to beat Alavés and Charlton, too. It was an incredible ending. This is a great time to be a Liverpool player, but then it's always a good time because this is such a fantastic club. Liverpool won a lot in the past and everybody was keen to bring the glory days back."

EMILE HESKEY

"It goes without saying I really enjoyed the season, but I'm hoping the best times are still to come. After the good start I did go through a bit of a barren spell in front of goal but I can honestly say I wasn't affected. I just knew I had to keep working in training and contributing to the team. I suppose the fact goals were flowing for me earlier in the season did silence a few critics but I don't have anything to prove to people outside the club. I've proved I can score on the big stage and that means a lot to me.

"It's not about me, though, it's about the team. Everyone here talks about the team ethic and not one word is a lie. We all respect each other, there's great camaraderie and we'll run ourselves into the ground to get the right result. I'm really happy at Anfield – I'm enjoying my game, I'm playing for an excellent team and I know I have a chance to realise all of my footballing ambitions."

ROBBIE FOWLER

"Since Christmas the games came thick and fast, but you'd rather have it that way than the season before when we only played 46 matches. Even so, finishing in a Champions League spot was always the priority. The manager said even if we won all three cups, the season wouldn't be a success unless we were also in the top three and the players all felt the same.

"Some people will always write you off when things don't go well, but I listened to the gaffer, worked hard and it paid off. I also had the fans behind me and they've been magnificent. That's why it was so special to score in the Worthington Cup final. I was so proud to be captain of Liverpool and lift the trophy that day. It was something I've always dreamt of. Winning that was a platform for even better things. We all felt we were going places."

NICK BARMBY

"To come to Liverpool, win three cups and be involved in all the other games in my first season has been brilliant. Every time I come to Anfield I think, 'This is brilliant, I'm playing for Liverpool!' Quite a lot of the lads feel the same. Jari Litmanen, Vladi and Markus were always fans.

"When I joined, the manager told all the players this season was going to be a building process and the aim was to go one better than last year. When you do that and win trophies, it shows you're going in the right direction. The manager has a two or three-year plan, the key to which is keeping this team together.

"I've played upfront and in midfield, wide right and wide left but I'll play where I'm put and I think I'm versatile. The boss likes players who are versatile and it increases your chances of getting a game if you can fill different roles."

STEVEN GERRARD

"At the start of the season we did let ourselves down at times but the team have performed well, the results have improved and ending it with three trophies and a place in the Champions League represents a very good campaign. We're desperate for success and we know the best way to achieve that is to maintain an excellent team spirit on and off the field. The manager has taken this club forward in a big way over the last year or so and the next step is to challenge strongly for the title.

"Personally, I received a lot of praise and won a couple of awards, which was fantastic, but at this club you can never afford to get carried away. The staff are great for keeping your head out of the clouds. I haven't found it a problem, though, as I'm a level-headed lad and I certainly don't have a big ego. When people don't want to talk about me, that'll be the time to worry."

SANDER WESTERVELD

"Manchester United were dominating the League long before I came to Anfield, just as they did this year. The way they operate is they don't buy many players during the season which means they have a good, solid squad where everyone knows each other. This is what we're trying to do at Liverpool, but it can't be done overnight. New players need time to adapt. It's understandable.

"I think we have a really good squad and I'd be surprised if we brought in many more in the near future. I'm confident if this group sticks together we'll improve significantly and who knows, maybe we'll go on to achieve similar things to United. Like I say, they don't change their team much over a season, but when they do they still have a team that wins games easily. They not only have the respect of opponents, they also have the fear, like Ajax used to have in Holland. It counts for a lot."

JAMIE CARRAGHER

"I think defensively we were very good. We had a few dodgy moments in the early stages of the season, but we worked hard on the training field to eradicate those. As a result we looked far more solid as a unit and teams had to work hard to score against us.

"I think many people expected us to have a dip in form because we were playing two or three times a week, but that didn't really happen. We had the players to do what we did and we produced when it mattered. Also the team spirit within the camp is first-class and it shone through.

"But we need to keep improving and make sure we start next season well. We made some silly mistakes at the beginning of this campaign that cost us crucial points and you never know how important those dropped points are going to be at the end of the year."

GAMES AND GOALS 2000/01

Opta @ PLANETFOOTBALL.com

	PREMIERSHIP GAMES/GOALS	FA CUP GAMES/GOALS	LEAGUE CUP GAMES/GOALS	UEFA CUP GAMES/GOALS	TOTAL GAMES/GOALS
Pegguy ARPHEXAD	0/0	0/0	2/0	0/0	2/0
Markus BABBEL	38/3	5/1	4/1	13/1	60/6
Nick BARMBY	26/2	5/1	6/1	9/4	46/8
Patrik BERGER	14/2	1/0	1/0	5/0	21/2
igor BISCAN	13/0	4/0	4/1	0/0	21/1
Titi CAMARA	0/0	0/0	0/0	0/0	0/0
Jamie CARRAGHER	34/0	6/0	6/0	12/0	58/0
Bernard DIOMEDE	2/0	0/0	0/0	2/0	4/0
robbie FOWLER	27/8	5/2	5/6	11/1	48/17
Steven GERRARD	33/7	4/1	4/0	9/2	49/10
Dietmar HAMANN	30/2	4/1	5/0	13/0	53/3
Vegard HEGGEM	3/0	0/0	0/0	1/0	4/0
Stephane HENCHOZ	32/0	5/0	5/0	10/0	53/0
Emile HESKEY	36/14	5/5	4/0	11/3	56/22
Sami HYYPIA	35/3	6/0	6/1	11/0	58/4
Jari LITMANEN	5/1	2/1	2/0	2/0	11/2
Gary McALLISTER	30/5	5/0	5/0	9/2	49/7
Erik MEIJER	3/0	0/0	0/0	0/0	3/0
Danny MURPHY	27/4	5/1	5/4	10/1	47/10
Alan NAVARRO	0/0	0/0	0/0	0/0	0/0
Michael OWEN	28/16	5/3	2/1	11/4	46/24
Richie PARTRIDGE	0/0	0/0	1/0	0/0	1/0
Jamie REDKNAPP	0/0	0/0	0/0	0/0	0/0
Vladimir SMICER	27/2	5/1	6/4	11/0	49/7
Rigobert SONG	3/0	0/0	0/0	1/0	4/0
Steve STAUNTON	1/0	0/0	0/0	1/0	2/0
Djimi TRAORE	8/0	0/0	1/0	3/0	12/0
Grégory VIGNAL	6/0	1/0	0/0	0/0	7/0
Sander WESTERVELD	38/0	6/0	4/0	13/0	61/0
Stephen WRIGHT	2/0	1/0	1/0	0/0	4/0
Christian ZIEGE	16/1	3/0	4/1	9/0	32/2

PREMIERSHIP TABLE 2000/01

		PD	W	D	L	F	A	GD	PTS
1	Manchester United	38	24	8	6	79	31	48	80
2	Arsenal	38	20	10	8	63	38	25	70
3	Liverpool	38	20	9	9	71	39	32	69
4	Leeds United	38	20	8	10	64	43	21	68
5	Ipswich Town	38	20	6	12	57	42	15	66
6	Chelsea	38	17	10	11	68	45	23	61
7	Sunderland	38	15	12	11	46	41	5	57
8	Aston Villa	38	13	15	10	46	43	3	54
9	Charlton Athletic	38	14	10	14	50	57	-7	52
10	Southampton	38	14	10	14	40	48	-8	52
11	Newcastle United	38	14	9	15	44	50	-6	51
12	Tottenham Hotspur	38	13	10	15	47	54	-7	49
13	Leicester City	38	14	6	18	39	51	-12	48
14	Middlesbrough	38	9	15	14	44	44	0	42
15	West Ham United	38	10	12	16	45	50	-5	42
16	Everton	38	11	9	18	45	59	-14	42
17	Derby County	38	10	12	16	37	59	-22	42
18	Manchester City	38	8	10	20	41	65	-24	34
19	Coventry City	38	8	10	20	36	63	-27	34
20	Bradford City	38	5	11	22	30	70	-40	26

GOALS SCORED

- ● Outside the box
- ● Inside the box
- ● Penalties
- ● Free-kicks

SCORED — HOME — CONCEDED
SCORED — AWAY — CONCEDED
SCORED — OVERALL — CONCEDED

YESSS! WHEN WE SCORE AT HOME

DOH! WHEN WE CONCEDE AT HOME

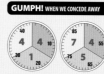

GERRIN! WHEN WE SCORE AWAY

GUMPH! WHEN WE CONCEDE AWAY

LIVERPOOL FC PLAYER CAREER STATISTICS

PLAYER / BIRTHPLACE/DATE OF BIRTH	PREMIERSHIP GAMES	GOALS	FA CUP GAMES	GOALS	LEAGUE CUP GAMES	GOALS	EUROPEAN GAMES	GOALS	LIVERPOOL GAMES	GOALS	CAREER GAMES	GOALS
Pegguy ARPHEXAD Abymes, Guadeloupe 18/5/73	0 26	0 0	0 4	0 0	2 4	0 0	0 0	0 0	2	0	36	0
Markus BABBEL Munich, Germany 8/9/72	38 242	3 8	5 0	1 0	4 0	1 0	13 49	1 5	60	6	351	19
Nick BARMBY Hull 11/2/74	26 245	2 46	5 28	1 9	6 17	1 5	9 0	4 0	46	8	336	68
Patrik BERGER Prague, Czech Rep 10/11/73	125 114	27 28	7 0	0 0	10 0	2 0	19 14	4 2	161	33	289	63
Igor BISCAN Zagreb, Croatia 4/5/78	13 65	0 9	4 0	0 0	4 0	1 0	0 9	0 0	21	1	95	10
Jamie CARRAGHER Liverpool 28/1/78	126	2	10	0	13	0	19	0	168	2	168	2
Bernard DIOMEDE Saint-Doulchard, France 23/1/74	2 175	0 30	0 0	0 0	0 0	0 0	2 21	0 5	4	0	200	35
Robbie FOWLER Liverpool 9/4/75	226	117	24	12	32	27	31	11	313	167	313	167
Steven GERRARD Liverpool 30/5/80	74	8	6	1	4	0	10	2	94	11	94	11
Dietmar HAMANN Waldasson, Germany 27/8/73	58 128	3 10	7 7	1 1	5 1	0 0	13 23	0 1	83	4	242	16
Vegard HEGGEM Trondheim, Norway 13/7/75	54 52	3 5	1 0	0 0	4 0	0 0	6 25	0 3	65	3	142	11
Stephane HENCHOZ Billens, Switzerland 7/9/74	61 203	0 3	7 7	0 0	8 4	0 0	10 9	0 0	86	0	316	3
Emile HESKEY Leicester 11/1/78	48 154	17 40	5 11	5 0	4 27	0 6	11 2	3 0	68	25	262	71
Sami HYYPIA Porvoo, Finland 7/10/73	73 163	5 11	8 0	0 0	8 0	1 0	11 13	0 0	100	6	276	17
Frode KIPPE Oslo, Norway 17/1/78 on loan to Stoke City	0 66	0 3	0 0	0 0	1 1	0 0	0 4	0 0	1	0	72	3
Jari LITMANEN Lahti, Finland 20/2/71	5 311	1 144	2 0	1 0	2 0	0 0	2 54	0 24	11	2	376	170
Gary McALLISTER Motherwell 25/12/64	30 551	5 98	5 38	0 9	5 52	0 12	9 8	2 3	50	7	698	129
Layton MAXWELL St Asaph 3/10/79 on loan to Stockport	0 19	0 1	0 1	0 0	1 2	1 0	0 0	0 0	1	1	23	2
Danny MURPHY Chester 18/3/77	67 150	7 28	8 7	1 4	9 7	7 0	11 0	1 0	95	16	259	48
Alan NAVARRO Liverpool 31/5/81 on loan to Crewe Alexandra	0 4	0 1	0 0	0 0	0 0	0 0	0 0	0 0	0	0	4	1
Michael OWEN Chester 14/12/79	123	64	8	5	10	7	21	7	162	83	162	83
Jorgen NIELSEN Nykabing, Denmark 6/5/71	0 0	0 0	0 0	0 0	0 0	0 0	0 0	0 0	0	0	0	0
Richie PARTRIDGE Dublin 12/9/80 on loan to Bristol Rovers	0 4	0 1	0 0	0 0	1 0	0 0	0 0	0 0	1	0	5	1
Jamie REDKNAPP Barton-on-Sea 25/6/73	233	29	18 3	2 0	26 3	5 0	23 0	3 0	300	39	319	39
Vladimir SMICER Degin, Czech Rep 24/5/73	48 172	3 42	7 0	1 0	8 0	4 0	11 23	0 4	74	8	269	54
Djimi TRAORE Laval, France 1/3/80	8 5	0 0	0 0	0 0	3 0	0 0	3 0	0 0	14	0	19	0
Grégory VIGNAL Montpellier, France 19/7/81	6	0	1 0	0 0	0 0	0 0	0 0	0 0	7	0	7	0
Sander WESTERVELD Enschede, Holland 23/10/74	74 115	0 0	8 0	0 0	5 0	0 0	13 4	0 0	100	0	219	0
Stephen WRIGHT Liverpool 8/2/80	2 3	0 0	1 0	0 0	1 0	0 0	0 0	0 0	4	0	28	0
Christian ZIEGE Berlin, Germany 1/2/72	16 240	1 51	3 1	0 0	3 1	1 0	9 31	0 6	32	2	308	60

Player stats and Premiership table for 2000/01 season. Figures in orange indicate games played for other clubs.

OPTA'S PLAYER BY PLAYER PREMIERSHIP STATS

Opta @ PLANETFOOTBALL.com

	Markus BABBEL	Nick BARMBY	Patrik BERGER	Igor BISCAN	Jamie CARRAGHER	Bernard DIOMEDE	Robbie FOWLER	Steven GERRARD	Dietmar HAMANN	Vegard HEGGEM	Stephane HENCHOZ	Emile HESKEY	Sami HYYPIA	Jari LITMANEN	Gary McALLISTER	Eric MEIJER	Danny MURPHY	Michael OWEN	Vladimir SMICER	Rigobert SONG	Steve STAUNTON	Djimi TRAORE	Gregory VIGNAL	Stephen WRIGHT	Christian ZIEGE
TIME ON PITCH	3,355	1,838	895	648	2,691	108	1,563	2,529	2,333	48	2,851	2,694	3,150	334	1,926	41	1,378	1,787	1,503	270	9	695	392	59	985
GOAL ATTEMPTS																									
GOALS	3	2	2	0	0	0	8	7	2	0	0	14	3	1	5	0	4	16	2	0	0	0	0	0	1
SHOT ON TARGET	6	8	8	4	3	1	25	23	10	0	0	43	12	5	13	1	10	42	11	0	0	0	0	0	4
SHOT OFF TARGET	13	15	14	6	4	0	26	27	26	0	1	39	10	2	11	0	13	28	21	0	2	0	1	0	12
BLOCKED SHOTS	2	6	7	3	3	0	11	15	22	0	0	30	3	4	6	0	6	12	10	1	0	0	0	0	4
PASSING																									
GOAL ASSIST	3	3	5	0	0	0	3	2	3	0	0	4	1	0	5	0	4	3	9	0	0	0	0	1	2
TOTAL PASSES	1,410	761	310	275	1,212	23	534	1,476	1,361	29	953	850	1,358	186	1,013	12	669	404	667	70	4	256	178	32	397
PASS COMPLETION	72%	73%	66%	66%	72%	78%	66%	72%	79%	69%	80%	69%	74%	74%	76%	75%	69%	72%	69%	54%	75%	63%	62%	72%	67%
CROSSING																									
TOTAL CROSSES	93	56	21	3	40	11	28	91	29	6	0	45	3	14	184	0	45	23	102	8	1	9	8	0	64
CROSS COMPLETION	24%	21%	24%	0%	23%	36%	11%	21%	14%	17%	0%	16%	67%	29%	38%	0%	33%	39%	27%	38%	0%	11%	0%	0%	20%
DRIBBLING																									
DRIBBLES AND RUNS	89	61	17	35	34	4	52	76	55	4	11	90	22	7	48	0	46	103	101	5	0	11	9	2	31
DRIBBLE COMPLETION	81%	80%	76%	54%	85%	50%	62%	78%	84%	50%	100%	61%	86%	57%	69%	0%	63%	48%	68%	60%	0%	73%	89%	100%	68%
DEFENDING																									
TACKLES MADE	87	58	24	21	95	2	19	128	114	3	91	51	93	6	48	3	58	28	48	13	1	27	21	1	30
TACKLES WON	67%	62%	88%	67%	81%	50%	74%	69%	76%	67%	80%	80%	69%	83%	75%	33%	81%	71%	60%	85%	0%	67%	76%	100%	87%
BLOCKS	9	1	3	2	13	0	0	10	10	0	41	5	28	0	9	0	2	1	1	1	0	7	1	1	7
CLEARANCES	218	11	4	4	188	0	3	63	37	1	275	44	466	0	34	0	15	3	9	14	0	40	23	1	35
INTERCEPTIONS	9	5	1	4	16	0	2	18	13	0	13	3	16	0	5	0	4	1	3	1	0	3	6	0	9
DISCIPLINE																									
FOULS	48	19	14	18	36	6	16	49	49	0	42	76	29	3	25	2	16	21	29	6	0	9	10	1	16
OFFSIDE	1	13	5	0	1	1	22	5	1	0	0	44	0	3	2	0	3	34	9	0	0	0	0	0	1
YELLOW CARDS	6	3	1	1	6	2	0	4	5	0	3	4	0	1	1	0	1	0	2	2	0	1	2	0	3
RED CARDS	0	0	0	1	0	0	0	1	1	0	0	0	0	0	0	1	0	0	0	0	0	0	0	0	0

SANDER'S STATS

TIME ON PITCH	3,420
GOALS	
GOALS CONCEDED	39
CLEAN SHEET	14
SAVES	
INSIDE BOX	55
OUTSIDE BOX	67
SAVES TO SHOTS RATIO	76%
CATCHES	
PUNCHES	29
CATCHES	71
DROPPED CATCHES	3
CATCHES SUCCESS RATE	96%
LONG DISTRIBUTION	
LONG KICKING DISTRIBUTION	1,036
SUCCESS RATE	51%
SHORT DISTRIBUTION	
THROW/SHORT KICKS ATTEMPTED	170
SUCCESS RATE	85%
DISCIPLINE	
FOULS	2
YELLOW CARDS	1
RED CARDS	0

★ STAR MAN

CARRY ON PLAYING
Of the outfield players, only our no6 started every league game. With Sander, he spent more time on the pitch than any other team-mate, his 3,355 minutes adding up to almost two-and-a-half days of solid football.

★ STAR MAN

SHOOT TO THRILL
Back to his best, Michael Owen was the club's top scorer in the Premiership with 16 goals from 28 appearances. He was also the team's most accurate and prolific shooter, trying his luck every 21.79 minutes that he was on the pitch.

★ STAR MAN

PASS MASTERS
Midfield maestro Steven Gerrard made the most passes (1,476) – an average of 52 per game – and almost three-quarters found their target. Only Didi Hamann of the big passers was more successful. Gerrard supplied the fourth most crosses (91) behind Gary Mac (184), Smicer (102) and Babbel 93.

★ STAR MAN

RUNNERS AND RIDERS
Vladi made over 100 dribbles and runs and supplied the second most crosses (102), but his cross-completion rate was just 27 per cent. However, he still claimed the most assists (9) ahead of Czech team-mate Patrik Berger (5).

★ STAR MAN

THEY SHALL NOT PASS
At the back, Stephane Henchoz made the most blocks (41) while Sami Hyypia made a phenomenal 466 clearances. Steven Gerrard just edged it over Hamann as best defensive midfielder with 128 tackles and 18 interceptions.

★ STAR MAN

THE TARGET MEN
Liverpool's no8 had a total of 43 shots on target during the Premiership campaign, the highest among the club's strikers, and 39 off target. Emile also scored the most blocked efforts with 30 shots, making it a great first full season.

THE FULL STORY

KEY

- ● Game Played
- ○ Substitute
- ● Goal Scored

Players

1	Sander WESTERVELD
2	Stephane HENCHOZ
3	Christian ZIEGE
4	Rigobert SONG
5	Steve STAUNTON
6	Markus BABBEL
7	Vladimir SMICER
8	Emile HESKEY
9	Robbie FOWLER
10	Michael OWEN
11	Jamie REDKNAPP
12	Sami HYYPIA
13	Danny MURPHY
14	Vegard HEGGEM
15	Patrik BERGER
16	Dietmar HAMANN
17	Steven GERRARD
18	Erik MEIJER
19	Pegguy ARPHEXAD
20	Nick BARMBY
21	Gary McALLISTER
22	Titi CAMARA
23	Jamie CARRAGHER
24	Bernard DIOMEDE
25	Igor BISCAN
26	Jorgen NIELSEN
27	Gregory VIGNAL
28	Richie PARTRIDGE
29	Stephen WRIGHT
30	Djimi TRAORE
31	Frode KIPPE
32	Jon NEWBY
33	Alan NAVARRO
37	Jari LITMANEN

Fixtures

DATE	H/A	OPPONENTS	RES	ATT	POS
Sat Aug 19	H	Bradford City	1-0	44,183	7
Mon Aug 21	A	Arsenal	0-2	38,014	11
Sat Aug 26	A	Southampton	3-3	15,202	12
Wed Sept 6	H	Aston Villa	3-1	43,360	5
Sat Sept 9	H	Manchester City	3-2	44,692	4
Thur Sept 14	A	Rapid Bucharest (Uefa 1/1)	1-0	12,000	
Sun Sept 17	A	West Ham United	1-1	25,998	4
Sat Sept 23	H	Sunderland	1-1	44,713	4
Thur Sept 28	H	Rapid Bucharest (Uefa 1/2)	0-0	37,954	
Sun Oct 1	A	Chelsea	0-3	34,966	7
Sun Oct 15	A	Derby County	4-0	30,532	4
Sat Oct 21	H	Leicester City	1-0	44,395	3
Thur Oct 26	H	Slovan Liberec (Uefa 2/1)	1-0	29,662	3
Sun Oct 29	H	Everton	3-1	44,718	3
Wed Nov 1	H	Chelsea (WC 3)	2-1	29,370	
Sat Nov 4	A	Leeds United	3-4	40,055	4
Thur Nov 9	A	Slovan Liberec (Uefa 2/2)	3-2	6,808	
Sun Nov 12	H	Coventry City	4-1	43,701	4
Sun Nov 19	A	Tottenham Hotspur	1-2	36,036	4
Thur Nov 23	A	Olympiakos (Uefa 3/1)	2-2	43,855	
Sun Nov 26	A	Newcastle United	1-2	51,949	5
Wed Nov 29	A	Stoke City (WC 4)	8-0	27,109	
Sat Dec 2	H	Charlton Athletic	3-0*	43,515	4
Thur Dec 7	H	Olympiakos (Uefa 3/2)	2-0	35,484	
Sun Dec 10	H	Ipswich Town	0-1	43,509	6
Wed Dec 13	H	Fulham (WC 5)	3-0	20,144	
Sun Dec 17	A	Manchester United	1-0	67,533	5
Sat Dec 23	H	Arsenal	4-0	44,144	4
Tue Dec 26	A	Middlesbrough	0-1	34,606	

Date		Opponent	Score	Attendance	
Mon Jan 1	H	Southampton	2-1	38,474	5
Sat Jan 6	H	Rotherham United (FA 3)	3-0	30,689	
Wed Jan 10	A	Crystal Palace (WC sf 1)	1-2	25,933	
Sat Jan 13	A	Aston Villa	3-0	41,336	5
Sat Jan 20	H	Middlesbrough	0-0	43,042	4
Wed Jan 24	H	Crystal Palace (WC sf 2)	5-0	41,854	
Sat Jan 27	A	Leeds United (FA 4)	2-0	37,108	
Wed Jan 31	A	Manchester City	1-1	34,629	4
Sat Feb 3	H	West Ham United	3-0	44,045	3
Sat Feb 10	A	Sunderland	1-1	47,533	3
Thur Feb 15	A	Roma (Uefa 4/1)	2-0	59,718	
Sun Feb 18	H	Manchester City (FA 5)	4-2	36,231	
Thur Feb 22	H	Roma (Uefa 4/2)	0-1	43,688	
Sun Feb 25	H	Birmingham C (WC f)	1-1†	73,500	
Sat Mar 3	A	Leicester City	0-2	21,924	4
Thur Mar 8	A	Porto (Uefa qf 1)	0-0	21,150	
Sun Mar 11	A	Tranmere Rovers (FA qf)	4-2	16,334	
Thur Mar 15	H	Porto (Uefa qf 2)	2-0	40,502	
Sun Mar 18	H	Derby County	1-1	43,362	6
Sat Mar 31	H	Manchester United	2-0	44,806	4
Thur Apr 5	A	Barcelona (Uefa sf 1)	0-0	90,000	
Sun Apr 8	H	Wycombe Wanderers (FA sf)	2-1	40,037	
Tue Apr 10	A	Ipswich Town	1-1	23,504	5
Fri Apr 13	H	Leeds United	1-2	44,116	6
Mon Apr 16	A	Everton	3-2	40,260	5
Thur Apr 19	H	Barcelona (Uefa sf 2)	1-0	44,203	5
Sun Apr 22	H	Tottenham Hotspur	3-1	43,547	5
Sat Apr 28	A	Coventry City	2-0	23,063	5
Tue May 1	A	Bradford City	2-0	22,057	3
Sat May 5	H	Newcastle United	3-0	44,363	3
Tue May 8	H	Chelsea	2-2	43,588	3
Sat May 12		Arsenal (FA Cup final)	2-1	72,500	
Wed May 16		Alavés (Uefa Cup final)	5-4*	65,000	
Sat May 19	A	Charlton Athletic	4-0	20,043	3

*own goal †Liverpool won 5-4 on penalties a.e.t

THE ANFIELD EXPERIENCE AT YOUR LOCAL NEWSAGENT

THE AWARD-WINNING* OFFICIAL LIVERPOOL MATCHDAY MAGAZINE
ON SALE EVERY MATCHDAY AT ALL GOOD NEWSAGENTS
ALSO AVAILABLE AT ANFIELD

*Voted Magazine of the Year at the 2001 PPA Awards for Editorial and Publishing Excellence